THE RESOURCEFUL TEACHER'S

Daniel Martín

activities for INTERACTIVE WHITEBOARDS

The author would like to express his gratitude to:

- Lucia Astuti at Helbling Languages for giving me the opportunity to publish this book.

- Jane Arnold for her enthusiasm from the very early stages and constant help in the editing process.

- Caroline Petherick for her outstanding editing work.

- Janett Walker for being a source of inspiration and a teacher with human touch.

Activities for Interactive Whiteboards
by Daniel Martín

© HELBLING LANGUAGES 2009
www.helblinglanguages.com

All rights reserved; no part of this publication may be reproduced, stored in a retrieval system, or transmitted in any form or by any means, electronic, mechanical, photocopying, recording, or otherwise, without the prior written permission of the Publishers.

First published 2009
ISBN 978-3-85272-148-4

Edited by Jane Arnold
Copy edited by Caroline Petherick
Designed by Gabby Design
Cover by Capolinea
Illustrations by Roberto Battestini
Printed by Bieffe

Every effort has been made to trace the owners of any copyright material in this book. If notified, the publisher will be pleased to rectify any errors or omissions.

Contents

The heart of the matter: interactive whiteboards — 6
A revolution in education — 6
A balanced approach — 7
What interactive whiteboards can do for you — 9
How to use the activities — 11

CHAPTER 1: IMAGE-BASED ACTIVITIES

Introduction — 17
1.1 A day in the life of … — 19
1.2 A story in pictures — 20
1.3 Associations — 21
1.4 At a restaurant — 23
1.5 Blind date — 25
1.6 Connections — 27
1.7 Face to face — 29
1.8 Find the differences — 30
1.9 Flashing pictures — 31
1.10 Going, going, gone! — 32
1.11 Going places — 34
1.12 Happy birthday to you! — 36
1.13 Horsing around — 38
1.14 How do I get to … ? — 40
1.15 How often? — 41
1.16 In the picture — 43
1.17 Life in 2050 — 44
1.18 Mime the picture — 46
1.19 More than meets the eye — 48
1.20 Most treasured possession — 49
1.21 My ideal classroom — 51
1.22 Out and about — 52
1.23 Picture dominoes — 54
1.24 Picture idioms — 56
1.25 Picture it — 58
1.26 Puzzled! — 59
1.27 Silent bingo — 60
1.28 Similar but different — 61
1.29 Stress patterns — 62
1.30 Tall – taller – the tallest — 63
1.31 The good side / the bad side — 64
1.32 The importance of English — 65
1.33 Unfolding story — 66
1.34 Weather report — 67
1.35 What's happening? — 68
1.36 What's in there? — 69
1.37 Where's Johnny? — 70
1.38 Wish you were here — 71

Contents

CHAPTER 2: SOUND AND VIDEO-BASED ACTIVITIES		Introduction	75
	2.1	Audio puzzle	78
	2.2	Breaking news	80
	2.3	Bubble story	81
	2.4	Concentration	83
	2.5	Controversial issues	85
	2.6	Disappearing lines	87
	2.7	DIY karaoke	89
	2.8	Every film tells a story	90
	2.9	Expanding stories	92
	2.10	Film dubbers	94
	2.11	Hummed greetings	96
	2.12	Intonation patterns	98
	2.13	It's football time	99
	2.14	Jumbled-up song lines	100
	2.15	Karaoke makers	102
	2.16	Moody sounds	104
	2.17	Odd words	106
	2.18	Reporting verbs	107
	2.19	Silent film	108
	2.20	Snakes and Ladders online news	109
	2.21	Sounds familiar	111
	2.22	Still frames	113
	2.23	Talking categories	114
	2.24	The newsroom	116
	2.25	Video auction	118
	2.26	Videoclip quiz	120
	2.27	Whose line is it?	122
CHAPTER 3: TEXT-BASED ACTIVITIES		Introduction	127
	3.1	Avid readers	129
	3.2	Flying places	131
	3.3	Fridge magnets	132
	3.4	From rags to riches	133
	3.5	Grammar ups and downs	135
	3.6	Google it	137
	3.7	Hiding lyrics	138
	3.8	Just joking	139
	3.9	Laser spelling	140
	3.10	Magic dictionary	141
	3.11	Moving phonemes	143
	3.12	Multiple-choice story	144
	3.13	Noughts and Crosses	146
	3.14	Once upon a …	148
	3.15	Personal profiles	149
	3.16	Personally speaking	151
	3.17	Pop lines	152

Contents

3.18	Predicting answers	153
3.19	Question, please	155
3.20	Sentence patterns	156
3.21	Song poems	157
3.22	Sounds like it	158
3.23	Taking sides grammar	160
3.24	Taking sides maze	162
3.25	Text puzzle	164
3.26	Top ten	165
3.27	Walk this way	167
3.28	What a holiday!	168
3.29	What's cooking?	170
3.30	What did Lydia do yesterday?	171

USEFUL RESOURCES 173

TEACHER'S QUICK-REFERENCE GUIDE 175

The heart of the matter: interactive whiteboards

A revolution in education

Laptops, wireless internet connection, mobiles, blogs, social networking sites, email accounts, satellite TVs, instant messaging, MP3 and 4 players, digital cameras, camcorders, online shopping, car navigation systems ... these are just some of the technological devices and breakthroughs that are part of our daily lives. They're part of the digital world we are living in – but it's one that we often leave behind when we enter the classroom. It must be admitted that as far as new technological advances and equipment are concerned the classroom has traditionally lagged behind other professional settings such as hospitals, offices and shops.

But the gradually growing provision and use of interactive whiteboards in education today opens new and exciting challenges. We, teachers and students both, can benefit from the integration of traditional teaching tools and new ones into a single piece of electronic equipment.

Overhead projectors, CD players and DVD players expanded the choice of visual and auditory teaching approaches. And now it is interactive whiteboards that are taking over the roles of not just those devices but also voice recorders and, last but not least, chalkboards. In addition to assuming all those roles, interactive whiteboards bring a new dimension to teaching, because all those devices are now integrated into a single unit that offers much better performance and helps us address a wider spectrum of learning styles simultaneously. In them, image, sound, word and motion blur, giving teachers the power to create lessons that can blend all those elements. The ground-breaking change in education we are witnessing today is the fact that we are able to produce not just text or sound or video or still pictures or pictures in motion – but fully-fledged interactive multimedia content.

As well as the benefits arising from the multiple applications of interactive whiteboards, their main advantage – and this is a must – comes from being connected to the internet. When you do that, you are bringing the outside world into your classroom. From visiting the British Museum to meeting a class of students from Japan. From instant access to thousands of teaching resources to browsing your students' blogs. From watching the latest video clip to setting up a karaoke party right away by directly accessing a karaoke page online. Anything that teachers can do and have been doing over the last few years with personal computers can now be done via the digital board for everyone to experience in a classroom setting on a big screen.

Digital boards bring real life into the classroom. Imagine that one of your students makes reference to something he/she just watched on the news. You can access a variety of online resources covering the issue in question (video or radio broadcasts, digital newspapers) or you may also find someone to chat and interact with outside your classroom. It all takes place instantly and spontaneously.

The divide between real and virtual is rapidly disappearing, and is in some cases difficult to establish. Is shopping online 'virtual shopping'? How about chatting with a so called 'virtual friend'? Digital boards become windows to the outside world and a platform for real/virtual hands-on experiences.

It is interesting that, in this sense, technology in general and the internet in particular can humanise textbooks, bringing a fresh approach to the topics and language covered in textbooks and supplementing them. Through the internet you can establish connections with those topics. You can motivate learners with authentic contemporary stories or experiences that are felt as 'real', unlike textbook material which is in many instances written ad hoc. Moreover, experiences gained through using the internet can bond people outside the classroom setting, enriching your students' lives and increasing their motivation to learn.

Another interesting aspect worth looking at, mostly when teaching teenagers, is that by incorporating interactive whiteboards and other technologies teachers are helping prepare their students for the many and varied challenges of the information technology era. In fact, one of the most popular directions of ESL teaching nowadays is CLIL, Content and Language Integrated Learning. By encouraging the use of technology in the English classroom, technology is accessed through English and English is accessed through technology. The students learn about the use of technology in English and then English is learned in practical ways by means of technology.

If interactive whiteboards can be a catalyst for a substantial number of learners who feel comfortable with this technology, identify with it and feel motivated by it, they can equally provide a strong incentive for us as teachers in exploring new territories, undergoing professional growth and tapping into our learners' interests. Research shows that once teachers become accustomed to this new tool, it would be hard for them to switch back to the 'old' teaching methods if they had to.

Finally, another equally significant aspect of top class education is that the information is no longer solely controlled by a unitary teaching authority but it comes from a sophisticated network of sources and is then shaped, reshaped and transformed. We as teachers will find ourselves stepping aside from playing the fountain of all knowledge in the classroom to becoming a guide and companion to learning. In many situations we will find ourselves relinquishing the control of the board to our students, who will have prepared beforehand multimedia work to be shared by the learning community.

A balanced approach

The ever-growing range of choices that the digital era offers can lead to confusion and feelings of being overwhelmed; too many changes brought into the classroom as a result of taking advantage of those new choices can then lead to erratic and inconsistent teaching practices. We should keep our eyes open for new teaching ideas, methods, tools and materials that can help us deliver our message more effectively; however, we need to keep things in perspective and constantly remind ourselves of the things that we are already doing well in class. In other words, we need to strike a balance between technology and tradition.

So ... what am I already doing well as a teacher? What are my strengths? Ask yourself these questions. Now, how can I use the digital board to enhance my lessons? How can I make my lessons even more stimulating and satisfactory? These, I believe, are crucial questions. Picture in your mind a learning situation in your classroom that does not originate from the board itself but that does make use of the board for further impact, attention span, effectiveness and overall enjoyment. Now, look at the different elements of your lesson and take some time to reflect on how you can incorporate the board into those existing elements.

The core question is not about what you can do with the board, but rather what the board can do for you. You need to be thinking in terms of how to blend the different multimedia components that can be incorporated into this tool to interact with each other and with other methodologies or teaching approaches you adopt. Showing text or pictures on the board or playing a listening extract or a video are not intrinsically interactive actions. But when performed with an interactive whiteboard, they bring a greater sensory impact and therefore, they provide added learning incentive. Combining the actions so that they support and enrich each other is interactive. It opens doors to finding creative ways, as the options presented by technology are wide and stimulating. The activities in this book contain ideas for interaction on the board between different multimedia materials adapted to other 'traditional' teaching ways.

An even more exciting and relevant aspect of interaction takes place among the learners themselves as a result of reacting to what is being presented to them. A strong emphasis has been placed in the activities in this book on learners being actively engaged in their use of the language in a collaborative environment. You will find movement in the classroom and the formation of groups is strongly encouraged. As technology, the internet and its multiplicity of personal learning environments allow learners to gain autonomy in their language acquisition you will need to create more time and opportunities in the classroom for learner interaction. On a personal level and looking back over my teaching career, I find myself teaching and talking less, and listening more. Interactive whiteboards are arguably the best electronic tool that teachers can possibly have in a learning environment today. But we still have our voices, our hands, jokes, songs, games, stories to share, movement in the classroom, student interaction …

The board is a companion to your repertoire and can both integrate your best teaching tricks and be integrated into them. In no way can the digital board replace the teacher. It needs to be operated somehow – and, deeper than that, there has to be some kind of rationale behind what you are doing on it. There needs to be content, and you, as a teacher, need to provide another equally important ingredient: context. Whether you have created the content or it comes from a CD-ROM you still need to warm things up, instil your sense of humour, rattle your students a bit, entertain, weave things.

It does take time and patience to learn and gain confidence. What makes you an effective user is not so much your technical ability or expertise but more your routine integration of the digital board into the regular pattern of classroom life. This doesn't imply that it should be used at all times. At some point, the board will no longer be seen as a novelty and your students will become engrossed in simply learning and interacting without even noticing the 'how', because they are focused on the 'what'. Interactive whiteboards, like any other electronic tools, would be irrelevant in the classroom setting without the learners and their emotions, needs and interests.

What interactive whiteboards can do for you

Ambience Interactive whiteboards can be used as excellent tools to provide ambience and a multi-sensory atmosphere by combining sound, still or moving images, colours and text to spice up your lessons and to make provision for the students' different multiple intelligences*. Improve your role-play situations by finding relevant pictures, videos or/and sounds that can instil added fun and motivation.

Authentic experiences Set up a video conference for your students to interact with another group of students 4,000 miles away – or perhaps with another English class just a few steps away in the same building. Check out breaking news online. Simulate the purchase of plane tickets. Visit the British Museum, or see what's happening at Times Square. Call someone on the phone over the internet. Post a video with students' presentations for the whole world to see.

Better presentation Use easy to see and read text fonts, diagrams, pictures and multiple word processing or project presentation tools to provide a more effective sensory impact.

Digital ways All newly published English courses offer a combination of paper and digital format that may include the following items: textbook, workbook, audio CDs, DVDs, CD-ROMs, internet links and digitalised textbook. On top of your own resources and educational materials, you can take advantage of the above items in the classroom and integrate them into your teaching practice.

Email Give your students the option of emailing you their homework assignments or posting their work in an online community group, a blog or a school webpage, and sharing these contributions with your whole class on the whiteboard. You may decide to assign work on a specific area for home reinforcement and open those emails in your next teaching session with a given group to review last day's teaching points.

Environmentally friendly You will find yourself supplying more material to your students but, ironically, using less paper and making fewer photocopies. Your students may also submit work digitally and take advantage of the digital platforms that may be in place for them, such as the internet, chat rooms, online community groups, school or class webpage, coursebook CD-ROMs, PowerPoint, etc.

Hyperlinking Increase the content and dimension of your lessons by hyperlinking – creating a link in your document on the board to another document that it can fetch from your pen drive, your computer or the internet. In this way, you can add sound, pictures, videos, web links, text or multiple combinations of the above elements to whatever your students can see on the board.

Improved visibility One of the most satisfying experiences in language classrooms equipped with interactive whiteboards is watching video material. The switch from TV set to wide screen board is a big and welcome change for your students. Close-ups of talking heads in the enhanced screen size give your students excellent examples for speech articulation as well, as it greatly facilitates word recognition. You may enlarge text size for everyone to see clearly and unmistakably. Large-sized pictures give you the chance to focus the attention of the whole class onto whatever language activity you have devised alongside the picture.

Internet Online dictionaries, chat rooms, karaoke sites, online magazines and newspapers, news on video, email access, ESL sites, Java applications, blogs, your own personal site, your school or class webpage, encyclopedias, course management systems, song lyrics, video sharing sites, film previews, wikis... Open a window to the whole world out there – and let your students take control while navigating from the board.

Maximising teaching time Interactive whiteboards maximise your teaching time by allowing you to move faster. Some of your material can be saved ready to show, and you simply retrieve it from a folder in your pen drive or computer, so there is no need to spend time writing or drawing. You may have different programs running – an electronic dictionary, a PowerPoint presentation and a specific site on your Web browser, and then switch back and forth from one to another as needed.

Modelling Scan samples of good work produced by your students to be displayed, or ask them to email you their work. You can mark them up with word processing applications – underline, circle, highlight, annotate, gap – to model your explanations. Another interesting way to model explanations is by using the screen recorder application. Save your document and use it again if needed, email it to your students or post it in a website for general access.

Motivation Many teachers find themselves revitalised and remotivated after experiencing the new dimensions and potentials for teaching inherent in this new technology. Pre-teens and teenagers find themselves identifying with a medium that is appealing to them and are more willing to be engaged in what they see as meaningful. This synergy has a positive spin-off effect onto classes.

Multimedia In the digital era, the dividing lines between picture, sound, word and motion have become blurred. With the interactive whiteboard you have the power to create multimedia lessons that combine any or all of the above elements and invite your students to come up to the front of the class and control the board. If you teach younger students, you'll know that they prefer learning through doing rather than just watching. The interactive whiteboard specially addresses the needs of young learners.

Portability No need to carry any electronic equipment to the classroom or teaching materials such as picture flashcards or board games. Everything can be stored in the computer or, better still, in a pen drive/flash drive.

This is even more comforting if you have to share your classroom with other colleagues.

Realia No need to find and physically bring to class real-life objects for your lessons. Run a picture search online for coins, cinema tickets, newspapers, football jerseys, restaurant menus, street maps, etc. Of course, you can still bring realia to class – but if you happen not to have it, you know it's always on the web. Additionally, you may share your holiday pictures with your whole class by showing them on the board. Your students can share what is important to them by showing pictures of their friends, their homes, their pets or their most treasured possessions. This way, it is easy to add personal meaning to the classroom.

Recycling The work produced during your lesson preparation sessions or generated in the classroom can be saved and used over and over again. This material can be modified if needed and saved again for immediate use with your next class or for longer-term use.

Resource bank If you are an experienced user, you will find yourself with an invaluable collection of internet educational links, software programs, coursebook digital materials, and the teaching materials generated by yourself and your peers – all ready to use by retrieving them from your files.

Unlimited display space Interactive whiteboards give you unlimited display space, as opposed to the physical restrictions of chalkboards. Additions are usually made by scrolling down the page to make room for them or by opening a new page, which also gives you the advantage of not having to erase existing information in order to display something else.

How to use the activities

Categorised activities The activities in this book have been classified into three categories – image-based, sound- and video-based, and text-based. However, the activities, whatever their category, do encompass a variety of sensory stimuli that can cater for different teaching approaches and multiple intelligences. There is a strong emphasis in this book on addressing different learning styles while taking advantage of integrating the different applications provided by the board. A quick-reference guide may be found at the back that allows you to search by focus, language level, estimated time of activity, and teacher's computer literacy.

Computer literacy As stated earlier, this is not a book on how to use an interactive whiteboard: a basic level of competency is required and assumed. Although some activities are more technically sophisticated than others, a strong emphasis has been placed on making the activities user-friendly, so that new users of the interactive board can feel confident. If you are an advanced user, you will find that you can add more sophistication to provide an even greater sensory impact. But whatever your degree of mastery, you will find activities suitable for you. The activities can also be saved, reused and refined as you increase in confidence, experience and proficiency.

Copyright laws Much teacher-generated material requires a search for online multimedia that will be used in class. Please observe the applicable copyright laws of your country and abide by the fair use doctrine. Some online material is protected under the Creative Commons licence, which means that only certain rights – or none – apply. Some activities suggest taking pictures of the students or recording short videos; if you are teaching underage students, make sure you get their parents' permission beforehand for these, stating that the electronic material will only be used for educational purposes within the classroom environment.

Flexibility The activities presented in this book are very flexible and contain easy-to-follow steps. However, they are open to modification for you to accommodate your students' needs or make room for your personal teaching style and preferences. By all means, do not follow to the letter the different steps in the activities presented if you can make changes or add something of your own creation to them which will improve them for you and your students. Ideally, these activities should be something inspiring which will encourage you to provide your own personal touch. You have the power to turn them into something unique and meaningful.

Group formation/pairwork The classroom setting is an ideal environment for students to exchange information and practise the language. Most tasks can be adapted so that students may work individually if the teacher wishes. However, group formation or pairwork is strongly advised. Additionally, students should be encouraged to work individually outside the classroom in order to gain as much exposure to the language as possible. You as teacher play a vital role here in providing customised guidance so that your students can benefit from technological advances in learning and practising the language.

Interaction The activities in this book promote interaction in the English classroom, both in the use of the board and between teachers and students in the classroom setting. Ideas to combine different sensorial elements on the board are given but, most important of all, interaction between the students themselves is promoted in the activities by incorporating pair work/group work or combining different language skills and multiple intelligences within the activities.

Internet Most of these activities do not require internet access in the classroom. However, an internet connection is needed for the activities that contain hyperlinks or ones for which you would like to use online material in the classroom. An internet connection allows use of streaming audio and video and instant access to relevant sites, which will give an added element of interaction and an invaluable connection between the classroom environment and the outside world. If you have an internet connection in the classroom, it is also a good idea to have a class blog, website, community group or a social networking site.

Language level You will find that the activities contained in the book address all language levels, from beginner to advanced. However, a strong emphasis has been placed on lower language levels, as most of these activities can be adapted to suit the learners' needs and language level.

Revision The activities presented may be adapted as a reinforcement of language matters already dealt with in class. You may also decide to print copies of the material on the board for your students, email it or even use the screen recording application.

Warming up Although in some instances suggestions have been made for warm-up activities, the teacher should ideally devise possible scenarios that can lead up to the activities contained in the book. Pique your students' curiosity and raise interest and excitement before you reach the focal point of your lessons. A crucial aspect regarding the student engagement and commitment that will lead towards the successful outcome of the activities lies in the manner in which you present them. Find authentic online material or student-generated material that can serve as a jumpstart to your lessons.

* Note
For practical activities addressing multiple intelligences which can be adapted for use in interactive whiteboards, see *Multiple Intelligences in EFL*, H. Puchta and M. Rinvolucri, 2005, Helbling Languages.

CHAPTER 1
IMAGE–BASED ACTIVITIES

Introduction

The visual impact of using pictures with interactive whiteboards is probably their most appealing feature. Colour photographs, drawings or any other kind of visual material can be shared and viewed on a big screen. Visual stimulus may be used to contextualise language and help learners prepare their minds and focus on certain topics or situations. Many standardised English tests require picture descriptions for the speaking section; the enhanced view provided by digital boards and the annotations that can be made on the screen can prove very helpful in preparing learners for that type of task. The main sources for pictures are the internet, the picture bank for the whiteboard software application and personal pictures from the teacher and learners.

The internet provides an overwhelming wealth of pictures that can be used as a springboard for description or discussion, to illustrate a related topic or to provide ambience. But when using it as a resource, do abide by fair use and observe applicable copyright regulations.

Google is likely to be the first resource that springs to mind for picture searches. A word search query typed into the search box followed by a click on the 'pictures' or 'images' link will probably prompt hundreds of options. It is also worth experimenting with the Advanced Search and Preferences features.

Another good source is Flickr (www.flickr.com), which offers a very comprehensive advanced search option, including a search for pictures made available under the creative commons licence; this is material that is made available to the public by their authors who have decided to waive – totally or partially – copyright restrictions.

The bank of pictures supplied by all the different software applications for the various whiteboard brands cannot be underestimated either. These pictures are categorised for easier access and the bank can be personalised by adding or deleting additional pictures from other sources. The array of pre-designed backgrounds is particularly convenient for classroom presentations.

By incorporating personal pictures, we can establish connections with the students' environment and we are opening doors into the classroom for what is relevant to them, such as family, friends, homes, pastimes or places. Many students will have digital pictures that can be emailed or stored on a pen drive and then shared in the classroom. The high level of emotional impact associated with personal pictures will be a catalyst for language activation, as learners will store – and retrieve – language more effectively when it has been made more memorable by the emotional tag attached to it.

There are several ways of inserting pictures into a document, but the easiest one is probably to copy and paste. Once you have found the picture you want to use, right click on it, select Copy from the pull-down menu, then go to the document page, right-click on it and select Paste. Once the picture is in the document, there are many editing features to be found in the various software programs for the different whiteboards, such a resizing, flipping, duplicating, fading, etc. A detailed look at the help files will allow you maximise these editing options.

A concept worth highlighting when working with pictures or

geometrical shapes is Object Layering; pictures or geometrical shapes – also referred to as objects – can be placed on top of each other. This is very useful because we can hide text behind an object, and then, by dragging the object, gradually reveal the hidden text.

Another equally interesting concept is Grouping. By dragging the area surrounding several items on the board with the virtual chalk or the mouse, we can group those items so that they become a single object. This means they can be moved around the screen together rather than one by one.

The tools in the different software programs vary in terms of number and performance, but all of them include a camera tool, which allows you to photograph the screen by a selected area, a window or the full screen. This particular feature is very useful when working with images.

It has to be acknowledged that looking for pictures that can spice up lessons and be meaningful and relevant is a time-consuming task. However, you can save those pictures and retrieve them for future use. Further, a vast array of prepared activities can be found online to download at no cost. If pictures are included, the content can be modified to adapt those activities to your needs or your students' language level. Many teachers are also willing to share their material with their colleagues, which is very helpful, especially for newcomers to the interactive whiteboard. At any rate, the time and effort invested will eventually pay off.

1.1 A day in the life of ...

Focus: Daily routines; sequencing events

Level: Elementary–Pre-intermediate

Time: 15 minutes

ICT skills: Copying and pasting pictures

Preparation:

1. Take some pictures of your personal daily routines, such as having breakfast at home, getting in the car, reading the paper, watching the news on television, teaching a class, walking the dog, etc.

2. Copy and paste those pictures to a page on the board in any order.

in class

1. Open the document you have created and explain that the pictures on the board show different daily actions of yours. In groups, your students discuss when those actions take place; tell them they should be constructing sentences using the present simple tense and sequencing those events (*first..., then..., next..., later on..., after that..., later..., finally...*).

2. Elicit answers from your students.

3. Put the pictures in order and tell them about your daily routine, providing additional information for each of your pictures.

4. Finally, your students, in groups, share their own daily routines.

Variation 1
Ask a student or group of students to email daily routine pictures to you, and follow the plan indicated above.

Variation 2
The same set of pictures can be recycled to introduce or review the past simple. *Yesterday I had breakfast at 8:00*, etc.

Variation 3
For Intermediate students, review the present simple or past simple tense, while placing a strong emphasis on the vocabulary needed to describe what is in the photographs.

A good relationship between students and teacher can be encouraged by sharing something of our lives with them.

1.2 A story in pictures

Focus: Encouraging speaking fluency

Level: Pre-intermediate–Advanced

Time: 15 minutes

ICT skills: **Option 1:** finding pictures online / scanning pictures; copying and pasting pictures to a page
Option 2: taking digital pictures; uploading pictures to the computer or pen drive, retrieving digital pictures and pasting them to a page

Preparation:
1. **Option 1:** Find a series of pictures that can shape a story (any number of pictures between five and ten seems to work well for this activity).
An online search for "picture stories" should gain good results. Copy and paste the pictures to a blank page and align them vertically. If the pictures are not isolated, use the Screen Capture application to separate them one by one.
Alternatively, scan some pictures from a book, magazine or newspaper, and paste them into a page as above.
Option 2: You – or your students – may use a digital camera to create a story in ten pictures. If your students have created the story, ask them to email you the pictures. Align them vertically on a blank page.

2. Open the screen shade/screen block application and cover all but the top picture on your page.

in class

1. Tell the class that they are going to see a sequence of pictures that illustrate a story. Tell them how many pictures are hidden on the board and say that you are going to reveal the pictures one at a time while allowing time for them to gradually construct a story based on the pictures visible.

2. Put your students into groups and let them construct the story as you drag the shade/screen block down to gradually reveal the pictures.

3. Once all the pictures have been displayed, invite students from all the different groups to share their stories.

Variation
Show all the pictures on the screen in a random order. Invite your students to make up a story using the pictures on the board. They may place the pictures in any order they wish.

Allow plenty of opportunities for creativity and let students savour it.

1.3 Associations

Focus: Contrasting and comparing pictures; formulating associations

Level: All

Time: 15 minutes

ICT skills: Finding pictures online; copying, pasting and resizing pictures on a page; dragging objects on the board

Preparation:

1. Find 12 to 20 pictures online that have no obvious connection to one another.

2. Copy and paste all your pictures onto a blank page. Scale down the pictures and place them on the lower third of the current page.

3. Bring any four pictures to the centre of the screen. Enlarge the pictures to maximise the view.

in class

1. Open the document you have created with the selected four pictures. Invite your students to describe the pictures.

2. Explain to your students that you want them to focus on the pictures and establish associations between any two of those four pictures. For example, imagine that you have pictures of a car, a shopping bag, a snow-capped mountain and a bird; you could give them these examples: *When I do my weekly grocery shopping, I drive my car to the supermarket and load up lots of shopping bags* and *I really envy birds: they get the best views of snow-capped mountains.*

3. Remove the pictures in the middle of the board and select four new ones from the bottom. Move them into the middle and enlarge them. Leave them there for one or two minutes. The students, in groups, spend a minute or two establishing associations between any two pictures displayed in the middle of the board, while you circulate to listen in and provide help with vocabulary.

4. When most groups have finished, go back to the board and elicit from some of the students their associations.

5. Repeat Steps 3 and 4 several times.

Variation
Place any four pictures in the centre of the board for your students to decide which of the four pictures has *no* connections with the

CHAPTER 1: IMAGE-BASED ACTIVITIES   21

1.3 Associations

other three. For example: *There may be lots of oil underneath that beautiful snow-capped mountain. Oil is used for making petrol for cars, as well as plastic for shopping bags. So the odd picture is the bird.*

Note
In addition to the picture bank provided in your board software, it is a very good idea to keep a picture bank in your computer or pen drive in order to have readily available teaching material.

Pictures evoke unique personal experiences which will, in turn, generate an unlimited number of associations.

1.4 At a restaurant

Focus: Language in situations: eating out

Level: Elementary–Intermediate

Time: 20 minutes

ICT skills: Taking pictures with a digital camera; uploading, copying, pasting and resizing pictures; printing saved documents

Preparation: Bring a digital camera to class.

in class

1. Introduce or review with your students key functional phrases used at restaurants.

2. Ask your students to close their eyes for a couple of minutes and imagine they are at a restaurant. While they have their eyes closed, ask them questions such as *What type of restaurant is it? What dishes can you smell? Is it busy? What are the people doing besides eating? What are they talking about? Where is the restaurant? Who you are sitting with?*

3. After two minutes, ask them to open their eyes again and share their mental images with a partner. Ask two or three students to share with the whole class as well.

4. Set up groups of three or four students and give them instructions to prepare a two-minute role play at a restaurant. One student in each group will be the waiter or waitress, and the remaining two or three will play the customers. Allow enough time for your students to prepare the role play and rehearse. Explain that they are allowed to take notes, but when they perform in front of other students it is better not to take the notes with them as the role play has a greater impact if notes are not used.

5. The groups, in turns, perform for the class.

6. Ask your class whose role play they liked the best. The most popular group will perform again. This time, take pictures of the highlights of the role play (seven to ten pictures will suffice) with your digital camera, to use for review (see below).

after the class

1. Upload the pictures to your computer. Retrieve the pictures and place them on a page on the board in the order that you took them.

2. Resize the pictures to fill most of the space on the board. Draw some speech bubbles next to the pictures.

1.4 At a restaurant

3. Save this document and print out copies for your students.

Review

1. Distribute copies of the handouts the next time you see your students as a review of the situational language.

2. Ask them to fill in the bubbles to recreate a conversation at a restaurant similar to the ones practised in class.

Variation 1
Use the handouts for a written English test where your students show their knowledge of the vocabulary and phrases they practised in class. They do not need to reproduce the role play that was presented in class. They simply need to prove they can produce relevant vocabulary for that specific task.

Variation 2
Devise any other situation where your students can actively practise key vocabulary (at a hotel, asking for directions, checking in at the airport, introducing themselves at a party, a job interview, etc.).

I hear I forget, I see I remember, I do I understand. (Chinese proverb)

1.5 Blind date

Focus: Encouraging oral fluency

Level: Intermediate–Advanced

Time: 30–40 minutes

ICT skills: Finding pictures online; copying and pasting pictures to a blank document; browsing for information on the internet.

Preparation:

1. Find pictures online of three female and three male fictional characters. The fictional characters suggested for this lesson are Lara Croft, Pocahontas, Bridget Jones, Spiderman, Don Quixote and Homer Simpson, but you may choose any you like.

2. Copy and paste the pictures of the three female characters into one page. Copy and paste the pictures of the three male characters into another page. Number each set of pictures 1, 2 and 3.

3. Find information online about the characters you have chosen, (for suggested topics, see In Class, 4), and prepare two handouts; one with information on the female characters and the other with information on the male characters. Ensure each description has the character's name and the number you've given them. Adapt the reading difficulty to the language level of your students.

4. Make enough copies of your handouts for your class; your female students will get the female characters and your male students the male characters.

in class

1. Ask your students if they know what 'blind date' means; if not, explain. If you teach a class of adult students, you could ask them if they have ever been on a blind date or how it went. Ask them what the most popular ways of meeting people these days are.

2. Tell your class they are going to play a game based on the popular UK quiz show *Blind Date*. In this show three male or female contestants were asked questions by people of the opposite sex that they could hear but not see. Eventually, the contestants had to choose one of the interviewers for a date. You may find information on this show here: http://en.wikipedia.org/wiki/Blind_Date_(UK_TV_series). You can also access footage by running a search on www.youtube.com with the words "cilla black blind date".

3. Ask for three male volunteers. Place three chairs or desks in front of your board for them to sit on with their backs to the board. Tell

1.5 Blind date

everyone that you are going to show three female fictional characters on the board and they are not supposed to give away the identities to the three volunteers.

4. Give the rest of the students their handouts and tell them to read the information. Meanwhile, the three students in the front will have to think of questions to ask the class, as if they were in the show. Sit down next to these three students and help them list their questions, making suggestions guided by the information sheets you put together, such as: *What is your favourite means of transport? Do you like exercising? Tell me about your passions in life. What is your idea of a romantic date? Tell me about where you live. Tell me about your personality.*

5. Start the game. In turns, the three students at the front choose a question and the number of a female character they would like to ask the question to. Any female student in your class may respond to the question, role playing that particular character. In order to give everyone a fair chance to answer, no student is allowed to answer twice in a row. Decide how many rounds of questions you would like to have. When the question rounds are over, ask each of your three students which character they would choose for a blind date and why.

6. Repeat Steps 3, 4 and 5, only this time with three female students sitting in the front, a display with the pictures of the male characters, and your male students in the class answering the questions.

Extension
7. Set up groups in your class for your students to choose their own characters (fictional or real) and play the game again. Monitor them to make sure they are on track, and provide help if necessary.

Variation
You may prepare a set of questions that can prompt hilarious answers, depending on the characters you selected, and write the questions on the board, next to the pictures. Your students may think of other questions to add, come up to the board and write them down. In that case, resize the pictures to leave enough space at the bottom of the screen for writing the questions.

A relaxed atmosphere has a strong impact on learning.

1.6 Connections

Focus: Word associations; explaining how things are related

Level: All

Time: 20 minutes

ICT skills: Dragging objects on the board

Preparation: Write a selection of words or phrases that you would like to review in class with your students.

in class

1. Tell your students that you would like to review some words and phrases with them.

2. Write those words and phrases down on the left-hand side, leaving plenty of blank space on the board.

3. Ask your students to come up to the board and either draw a simple picture that could somehow have a connection or association with a word or phrase from the list, or write a word, phrase or connecting sentence. They can come up to the board as many times as they wish, but never twice in a row, thus encouraging varied class participation. Tell them not to explain their choice; they should simply leave their contribution on the board.

4. When you have sufficient contributions – perhaps 15 to 20 – ask your students to have a good look at them, and then invite the students to come up to the board, select one and drag it next to one of the words or phrases on the left. Let them know that they cannot select something that they wrote or drew themselves.

5. The student standing in front of the board must explain why they think that the picture or word, sentence or phrase that they have dragged has a connection. Then ask the student who made that specific contribution to confirm that this was the connection they had thought of, even if the explanation is different. If there is a connection, let them explain why they placed that drawing or word/s on the board, and leave the matched pair on the board. Otherwise, the drawing, word, phrase or sentence is dragged back to its original place.

6. Repeat Steps 4 and 5 until you run out of 'connections'.

Variation 1
Put pictures on the left-hand side of the board, instead of words or phrases.

1.6 Connections

Variation 2
You may personalise a reading comprehension passage displayed on the board. Choose something appropriate for your students´ level, and make sure you leave enough space on the screen for your students to draw or write their connections. Highlight key words or phrases in the passage, and let your students establish personal connections with the text.

Variation 3
Set up groups of three or four students. Tell them to choose one of the connections on the board for a group picture; that is, they will be coming to the front of the class to draw the picture on the board and pose with it for the rest of the students to try to guess which connection they chose.

Make accommodations for spatial intelligence: let your students create or think in images.

1.7 Face to face

Focus: Encouraging the asking of questions; physical descriptions

Level: Beginner–Elementary

Time: 15 minutes

ICT skills: Finding pictures online; copying and pasting pictures

Preparation:
1. Find 15 to 20 pictures of celebrities.
2. Copy and paste the pictures to a blank page, and insert name labels. Resize the pictures so they can all fit onto one page.

in class

1. Show your document to your students.

2. Model the activity. Explain that you are going to secretly select one of the pictures on the board and they are to ask yes/no questions to find out who the selected person is. The questions could be: *Is this person less than 30 years of age? Is it a man? Is he a singer? Does he have long brown hair? Is he wearing a green shirt?* etc.

3. Students work in pairs and, in turns, one secretly selects a celebrity and the other tries to guess who it is.

Variation
Put your students into pairs. In turns, they choose someone else in the classroom, and their partner asks yes/no questions to find out who the person is.

Contexts that narrow down the possible language outcome to specific language areas help students focus and retrieve the expected target language.

1.8 Find the differences

Focus: Describing pictures; talking about differences

Level: Beginner–Elementary

Time: 15 minutes

ICT skills: Duplicating objects

Preparation:

1. Use the upper half of the board to draw a picture which includes a variety of actions and objects.

2. Select the picture and copy it. Place the second picture on the bottom half of the page.

3. Select the virtual eraser and erase a few things from the second picture. Then select the virtual pen and bring some changes to it. For example, if the original picture showed a clear sky, add a few clouds to the second one. If the first picture showed a woman carrying a shopping bag, make her carry an umbrella this time.

in class

1. Show your class the document you have created. Ask your students, in pairs, to look at the board and talk about the differences between the first and the second picture.

2. After you have given your students a minute or two to compare the pictures, elicit the differences.

3. Ask for a volunteer to come up to the board, and make some changes, as you did in Preparation Step 3. Meanwhile, the rest of the students should look down or close their eyes.

4. Students, in pairs, compare the pictures again and find the new differences.

Variation
Ask for two or three volunteers to leave the classroom for a couple of minutes (or they can close their eyes). Tell the rest of the class to 'change things' in the classroom, that is, someone can put on someone else's sweater, you may turn on or off the lights, books may be placed on a desk, someone may remove her glasses, etc. After two minutes, the volunteers may come back to the classroom – or open their eyes – take a look around and state what changes have been made (Julio is wearing Mario's sweater, the lights are on now, there are no books on the teacher's desk now, Maria isn't wearing glasses now, etc.).

Interactive whiteboards let you create, store and retrieve a wealth of visual stimuli that can be quickly and easily manipulated to suit your teaching needs.

Flashing pictures

Focus: Basic vocabulary for indoor objects; *there is/there are*

Level: Beginner–Elementary

Time: 10 minutes

ICT skills: Copying and pasting pictures; screen shade application

Preparation:
1. Find three or four pictures – or draw them yourself – featuring plenty of everyday objects, for instance pictures of rooms, offices, classrooms, etc.
2. Copy and paste each picture to a different page on your board, and enlarge them so they can be seen clearly.

in class

1. Tell your students that you are going to flash a picture for them on the board. They must be very alert and then, in pairs or small groups, they should try to write down as many sentences as possible using the structures *'There is'* or *'There are'*, stating what there is in the picture.
2. Show your first page with the first picture in it. Quickly open the screen shade and cover the picture with it. Drag the screen shade down to reveal the picture and, after a few seconds, cover the picture again with the screen.
3. The students write down sentences stating what there is in the picture.
4. After a minute or two, ask your students to put their pens down, then you reveal the picture again and invite them to read out their sentences. You may also invite them to come up to the board and write their sentences down below each picture.
5. Repeat Steps 2, 3 and 4 with the rest of the pictures.

Variation 1
Modify the grammatical structures and practise the past tense, with *'There was'/'There were'*.

Variation 2
Choose pictures showing many actions, for your students to write down sentences using the present continuous or past continuous tenses.

Pictures may not always be worth a thousand words but they can be an invaluable source for vocabulary acquisition and drilling.

Going, going, gone!

Focus: Numbers 1,000–10,000,000

Level: Pre-intermediate

Time: 40–60 minutes

ICT skills: Browsing for pictures on the internet; copying, pasting and resizing pictures from a document

Preparation:

1. Find some famous paintings online (you could run a Google search with the names of the paintings or visit the websites of the world's most prestigious museums). Choose around 12 to 15 paintings.

2. Copy and paste those pictures onto a blank page. Scale them down and place them at the bottom of the screen. Write the word *Auction* at the top of the page.

3. Think of a price tag – a number between 1,000 and 10,000,000 – for each of the paintings (for instance €1,345,638, €779,390, €992,785, and so on). Those will be the starting prices for the bidding.

in class

1. Call out the phrase 'Going, going, gone!' in class. Elicit its meaning from your students. Ask them: *In which situation would you hear these words?* Now project the document you have created with the pictures on them and elicit – or explain – the meaning of 'auction'.

2. Set up groups in your class and explain that they will have to bid for those paintings as though they are at an auction. Every group has 10 million euros to spend and their aim is to try to buy as many paintings as possible with the money they have.

3. Bring one of the pictures from the bottom of the screen to the middle and enlarge it. Write down the price tag in numbers, then start the bidding. (You should be the auctioneer to begin with, but a confident student could take on that role later.) The auctioneer calls out the starting price and invites the groups to bid. Each bid should be written down on the board by a student. When nobody bids any higher, the auctioneer calls 'Going, going' gone!' and the painting is sold. Every time a painting has been sold, write the word SOLD over it, scale it down, drag it to one side and bring a new picture to the middle.

4. Every group will be responsible for keeping track of their money balance.

1.10 Going, going, gone!

Variation 1
With higher-level groups, you may ask your students to describe the paintings once the auction is over. Follow-up questions could be:
- What do you like about this painting?
- Where would you hang this painting in your house?
- Which one is your favourite painting? Why?
- Do you think you paid too much for your paintings?
- Has anyone seen any of these paintings before? Where?

You could also lead a general discussion about art.
Finally, you could ask your students to write separate answers to the above questions, or ask them to structure their answers as continuous text in paragraphs in their notebooks, language journals, online blogs, your webpage or in an email to you. Read some of the answers next day in class or, better still, show them on the board.

Variation 2
With elementary students you could review numbers 1–100 by using price tags such as €19.99, €31.55, etc. Tell them that they have €300 to spend. Instead of paintings, you may use, for instance, clothes, which will give you the opportunity to introduce or review relevant vocabulary at that level.

Make target language serve a real purpose. Create meaningful experiences that can engage your students.

CHAPTER 1: IMAGE-BASED ACTIVITIES

1.11 Going places

Focus: Functional language used when travelling by plane

Level: Elementary–Intermediate

Time: 20 minutes

ICT skills: Finding pictures online; copying and pasting pictures to different pages; enlarging objects

Preparation:

1. Find pictures online that recreate airport scenes, such as a traveller checking in, another traveller going through passport control, etc. Two search terms that should bring you good enough pictures to project in class are: "airport" + "check-in" and "airport" + "passport control".

2. Select one picture from each of your searches and copy and paste each to a different page on your board.

3. Enlarge each picture so that it takes up about three quarters of the page.

4. Write headings for both pages. The first page could be headed 'Checking In'. The heading for the second page could be 'Passport Control'. Choose a colour and font size that stand out from the background.

5. Select key functional language that you would like to introduce or review which is relevant to each of the travelling situations, and write it into the space at the bottom of each page. For instance, at Elementary/Intermediate level you could choose phrases such as:
   First page: *Can I see your passport, please? Here you are. Please put your bags on the scales. Aisle or window seat? This is your boarding pass. Enjoy your flight.*
   Second page: *What is the purpose of your visit? Where will you be staying? Anything to declare? Enjoy your stay!*

in class

1. Lead into the activity by asking your students if they have ever flown, when, where, what's the furthest distance they have ever travelled, and so on. Tell them that you are going to introduce – or review – functional language used when travelling by plane.

2. Show them the pictures and the key phrases on the board. Review the vocabulary with them and make sure they understand it. You could also ask them questions about the pictures, such as: *What's the man doing? What's the lady carrying? What's this man's job?* etc.

1.11 Going places

3. Set up pairs in class. If there is an odd number of students, pair with one of them.

4. Ask them to improvise dialogues based on the first page, using – among others – the expressions on the board.

5. Repeat Step 4 for the second page.

6. Ask for volunteers to come up to the front to share their dialogues.

Variation 1
For homework, ask your students to choose one of the situations, find a similar picture online and copy and paste it to a blank page. They should leave enough space at the bottom of the page to write a short dialogue. Ask them to email you this document as an attachment. Open the documents in class and share with your students.

Variation 2
Modify the functional language to adapt it to higher language levels.

Recreate locations and sets of real-life situations for a more enjoyable learning experience.

1.12 Happy birthday to you!

Focus: Encouraging off-the-cuff oral fluency

Level: Pre-intermediate–Intermediate

Time: 20 minutes

ICT skills: Finding pictures online; copying and pasting pictures to different pages; enlarging objects

Preparation:

1. Find a picture online of a birthday party; search for "house party" or "birthday party". Choose an image that is appropriate for the age of your students.

2. Enlarge the picture so that it takes up most of the space on the page, leaving space at the top, and copy and paste that picture onto six more pages.

3. Head each page with an instruction or task for your students, picking a text colour that ensures the heading is clearly visible. Suggestions:
   a) Arrive at the party. Greet everyone.
   b) Talk to someone about the present that you bought for the birthday party.
   c) You see an old friend. Talk to him/her about what you have been doing lately.
   d) Explain to someone why you almost didn't make it to the party.
   e) Explain to someone why you are having a great time/a boring time at the party.
   f) You have some exciting news about your school/job/friends to share.
   g) Time to say goodbye.

4. Create ample space in the room for your students to circulate and mingle.

5. Optional (see Step 3 below): a set of plastic cups and plates and some background music.

in class

1. Explain that it's your birthday today – which may or may not be true. Tell your class that you have decided to have a birthday party in class. Ask about whether they celebrate their birthday, what they do, whether they like birthday parties, etc.

2. Tell the students that they will see a picture on the board and seven different situations. As each new situation is displayed, they have to pair with someone else and engage in a conversation until

1.12 Happy birthday to you!

you display the next situation. Then they will have to find another student to have a conversation with and so on, just as if they were really attending a birthday party.

3. Display the pages one by one, leaving enough time for your students to interact. For better ambience, play background music and provide (empty) plastic cups and plates.

Variation
Feel free to choose other situations, or negotiate them with your students. You may host different parties during the school year and use them as an excuse to provide a relaxed and enjoyable atmosphere conducive to achieving speaking confidence and fluency.

Acknowledgements to John Hughes, from whom I devised this modified version of his board game 'At the Party'.

Provide pleasant experiences to foster a good working environment.

1.13 Horsing around

Focus: Reviewing idioms based on animals

Level: Intermediate–Advanced

Time: 30 minutes

ICT skills: Browsing the internet for pictures; setting up a grid pattern; copying and pasting pictures into that grid, and putting numbers into it; creating objects and dragging them; using a virtual die, virtual pen and virtual eraser

Preparation:

1. Find 24 animal-based idioms that you would like to review; you will need to have them in multiples of three, for example three horse-based idioms, six cat-based ones, three dog-based and so on.

2. Run an online picture search for the relevant animals.

3. Create a Snakes and Ladders style board-game grid with about 40 or 50 numbered squares, filling half a page. In eight of the squares, insert one of your animal pictures; there will three different idioms for each animal square.

4. Type your idioms into the blank half of the page.

5. Select the virtual pen and run it over each of the idioms, leaving visible the relevant animal word and – fully or partially – another word in each line, to provide a clue. For example, if the idiom in question is "straight from the horse's mouth", leave "horse's" and "mouth" visible. Or if the idiom is "to let the cat out of the bag", leave "cat" and "bag".

6. Create circles of different colours to use as counters for the game; the size of each circle should be about half the size of a grid square.

7. Check that you have a virtual die feature and you can use it; if not, provide a real die.

in class

1. Tell your class that they are going to play a board game to review idiomatic expressions based on animals. Set up three groups.

2. Explain the rules of the game:
   a) each group takes turns to throw the die (if you have the virtual die feature, use that application; otherwise use a real die).
   b) If a group's counter lands on a square with, say, a horse in it, they have to produce an idiom that contains that animal word. If their answer is on the board already, erase the ink covering

1.13 Horsing around

the expression. A correct answer gives them ten points. If they fail to produce a valid answer – i.e. either the idiom you have written on the board, or another one that fits – erase some more ink covering the line in question, to unveil an additional complete or partial – word. If they can produce a valid answer with that clue, give them five points.

3. Groups take turns moving their counter until they have all reached the finish square. The group with the highest score wins.

Variation 1
Centre your lesson around colour-related idioms, or body, clothes, food or money idioms.

Variation 2
For more advanced and adventurous users: hyperlink your answers to online dictionary definitions and examples.

Variation 3
Devise a class project where your students have to produce their own virtual idioms board game.

Games are enjoyed by people of all ages.

1.14 How do I get to ... ?

Focus:	Asking and giving directions
Level:	Elementary–Pre-intermediate
Time:	10 minutes
ICT skills:	Browsing online; superimposing drawn objects and writing onto them
Preparation:	1. Find a city map in an English-speaking country and select a section that has about ten streets running through it in each direction; download it onto a blank page.
	2. If it's a simple street plan, you might like to draw some spaces into it to indicate important buildings, such as school, cinema, church etc, and label them.
	3. Think of several routes through the streets that will challenge your students at an appropriate level.

in class

1. Introduce or review the key functional vocabulary and phrases that are used when asking and giving directions.

2. Show the city map on the board and ask for two volunteers to play the roles of a tourist and a city resident, as an example of how to do this activity. The tourist picks a location and a destination on the map and asks the resident to give directions from one to the other.

3. Select the virtual highlighter and mark a route on the map. Put your students into pairs and ask them to give directions following the highlighted route on the map.

4. Erase the route you marked and draw a different one. Your students switch roles.

5. Repeat Steps 3 and 4 a few more times.

Variation
Choose a location on the map and start giving directions from it to an undisclosed destination. Ask your students to tell you where you have ended up on the map.

When there is a will, there is a way. When there is no will, there is no way. Find ways to move your students' will to learn.

1.15 How often?

Focus: Adverbs of frequency

Level: Elementary

Time: 10 minutes

ICT skills: Looking for pictures online; copying and pasting pictures to a page; dragging objects on the board

Preparation:
1. Go online to find about ten pictures of actions; for instance, somebody playing football, reading a newspaper, drinking a cup of coffee, etc. Copy and paste the pictures to a page and place them in a row along the bottom quarter of the page.

2. On the upper three quarters of the page draw six columns, and head them with these frequency adverbs: *never, hardly ever, sometimes, often, usually, always*.

in class

1. Show the document you have created and ask your students what is happening in each picture *(she is playing football, he is reading a newspaper, he is drinking a cup of coffee*, etc.).

2. Invite a student to come up to the board and place the pictures in the different columns according to how often he/she does the actions shown in them. Ask your student to compose complete sentences using the frequency adverbs that head each column (*I sometimes play football*, etc.).

3. Repeat Step 2 a few more times, with a different student each time.

4. Then put the students into pairs, to compose full sentences using the frequency adverbs.

Variation 1
1. Choose one picture and drag it into the middle of the board. Tell your students: *Guess! How often do I ...* (followed by action in the picture)? (You may need to explain the meaning of 'guess'.) Elicit full sentences with your students using the frequency adverbs, and after every correct guess place the picture in the corresponding column.

2. Then invite a student to come up to the board so that the other students can guess how often he/she does the different things.

1.15 How often?

Variation 2
Other possible language structures for the action pictures could be: *I have never –ed; I have –ed; I like/dislike/enjoy/am not keen on/love/hate –ing; I can/I can´t.*

Manipulating images and relating language to personal experiences can help students learn more effectively.

1.16 In the picture

Focus: General speaking practice and interaction

Level: All

Time: 10–20 minutes

ICT skills: Taking digital pictures; uploading, retrieving and placing the pictures on a page

Preparation:

1. Take a digital picture of each of your students and yourself – or ask a student to take them. Create a folder in your hard drive or pen drive with subfolders for each of your classes, and save your pictures there.

2. Copy and paste the pictures of your students from a subfolder to a page. Include your own picture, too. Save that document for future use.

3. Decide on some topics from your current unit for your students to have brief conversations about.

in class

1. Drag the pictures onto the board and arrange them in pairs. If you have an odd number of students, use your own picture.

2. Ask your students to look at the board and pair off with the person whose picture is next to his/hers, and have a five-minute conversation about a topic from your current unit.

3. Ask a student to jumble up the pictures and drag them again to form different pairs.

4. Repeat Steps 2 and 3 as many times as you consider necessary.

Note
You or your students may have generated a set of relevant questions to address your current topic; the questions may be provided by your textbook or a worksheet. You may use this activity to review other units. The focus may be on functional language, or you may have created different role plays. You may use this student picture bank repeatedly when you want to pair off students or set up groups in class.

This is a motivating way to get your students busy and promote interaction in the classroom.

CHAPTER 1: IMAGE-BASED ACTIVITIES

1.17 Life in 2050

Focus: Future forms in English; research on life in the future; team presentations

Level: Intermediate–Advanced

Time: 60 minutes

ICT skills: Copying and pasting information onto the board

Preparation: Have access to a language laboratory with internet connection for the entire class.

in class

1. Ask your students how they imagine life on this planet will be in the year 2050. How old will they be? What problems will the world be facing? Will it be a very different world? Better or worse? In what ways? Ask other questions that may be relevant to the class to stimulate their interest.

2. Divide the class into three or four teams, each team to be in charge of a specific topic such as *the environment, technology, energy resources* and *family life.*

3. Tell them that each team will then give an audiovisual presentation of five to ten minutes on their subtopic. It will not be necessary for everyone in the team to stand in front of the class to present, but each team needs at least two presenters, and the presentation should include a contribution from every team member. The presentation could contain text, pictures, videos, sound, graphs or/and drawings. Your students may use PowerPoint if they are familiar with it, or they can simply copy and paste the material to different pages on the board. They may save the material in a pen drive or email it to an account to be accessed in class.

4. Take your whole class to the language lab to do research on their topics. A few helpful search results should be prompted by typing "predictions for the future", "technology and the future" "energy resources in the future", "family life and future" and "life in 2050".

5. The different teams present their topics. Meanwhile, all the teams must think up at least one question to ask each presenting team. After all the teams have done their presentation, hold a debate with all the questions generated.

6. Ask your students to email to you – or write in their blogs – a brief summary of the presentations or some brief personal comments.

1.17 Life in 2050

Variation 1
Other possible cross-curricular issues:
- climate change
- profile of an English-speaking country
- profile of a music band
- world celebrations

Variation 2
You can introduce this activity at the end of a lesson, telling them to do their research at home or at a library outside class hours. Then the main lesson will be used for the presentations.

Approach English language learning through cross-curricular topics.

1.18 Mime the picture

Focus: Present continuous tense

Level: Beginner–Elementary

Time: 10–15 minutes

ICT skills: Finding pictures online; copying and pasting pictures to a page

Preparation:
1. Find pictures online of actions whose verbs you would like to review or introduce in class; these must be actions that can be performed by students in the classroom.
2. Copy and paste each picture to a different page.

in class

1. Mime an action to your class. For example, pretend that you are running. Ask your class: *What am I doing?* for them to answer: *You are running.*
2. Ask another student to think of an action and mime it for the class to guess.
3. Show them the page with the first picture. Ask everyone in the class to mime the action. Write below the picture a full sentence that refers to that action.
4. Tell your class that you have more pictures for them. Ask for a volunteer to come up to the front of the class and stand with his/her back to the board. Show the next picture. Everyone in the class mimes the action for the volunteer to make educated guesses orally until you decide he/she gets a valid answer, which he/she then writes on the board below the picture.
5. Repeat Step 4 several times, each time with a new picture and a new student.
6. When all your pictures have been displayed and the corresponding sentences have been written down, return to the first page and work through the pictures again, for the class to read the sentences aloud in unison with you.

Variation 1
Write down sentences to describe each of your pictures and hide them by placing a rectangle filled with colour over them. Then drag the rectangles to reveal the answers.

Mime the picture

Variation 2
After all the pictures have been revealed, use the virtual eraser to erase the verb in each of the sentences, and elicit it from your students.

Variation 3
Instead of using pictures, you could just write down sentences; this variation will take less time, as the students will only be miming and guessing.

Variation 4
You can adapt the exercise to higher levels by focusing on more complicated grammatical structures.

Movement increases brain and blood oxygenation, which improves learning conditions and language output.

1.19 More than meets the eye

Focus: Predictions (*may, might, could be, looks like*)

Level: Pre-intermediate–Intermediate

Time: 10 minutes

ICT skills: Finding pictures online; copying and pasting pictures; using the screen capture application

Preparation:
1. Find pictures online of everyday objects (a pair of glasses, a cup, a bicycle, a computer, etc.).
2. Open your screen capture application and select an area of each picture that you are going to place on the board. The selected area should partially reveal the shape of the object, for your students to be puzzled and make guesses, using *may, might, could be, looks like*.
3. Place the first part-picture on a page, and copy and paste the full picture to the next page. Do the same with the remaining pictures.

in class

1. Introduce or review with your class the key modal verbs and language used for making predictions. You may hide something in your hand and show a clenched fist for your students to say *It may be a coin; It might be a ring; It could be an eraser*; etc.
2. Show your students the first part-picture, and invite them to guess what the object in question might be. When a correct guess is made, move to the next page to show the complete object.
3. Repeat Step 2 with the remaining pictures.

Variation
Instead of objects, find pictures that can show actions for your students to make guesses, using the present continuous tense.

Everything you can imagine is real. (Pablo Picasso)

Most treasured possession

Focus: Question asking and general oral fluency; describing objects

Level: Pre-Intermediate–Advanced

Time: 20 minutes

ICT skills: Copying and pasting pictures to the board

Preparation:
1. Ask four to six of your students to email you – or bring to class in a digital format – a picture of their most treasured possession. They can also bring the object itself to class.
2. Copy and paste each picture to a different page on the board.

in class

1. Tell your class that some students have emailed you a picture of their most treasured possession. Show all the pages containing the pictures on the board.
2. Call the students who emailed the pictures, mixed with an equal number of students who did not email anything, to the front of the class. Call them up individually, by name; do not reveal whether or not each student has emailed a picture.
3. Ask the remaining students to think of possible questions they can ask about the pictures, such as: *Why does it mean so much to you? Where did you buy it? Who gave it to you? Is it worth a lot? Where do you keep it?* etc.
4. While most of the students in the class are writing down the questions, assign each of the objects to two students (one student being the actual owner and the other one from the group that did not send any pictures). Tell them all that whether or not they own the object in the picture, they should respond to the questions asked by the remaining students as if it was theirs.
5. Show the picture on the first page. Tell the class that it may belong to student A or student B. Encourage your students to fire the questions for both students to answer (one with the real information; the other one with made-up details).
6. Ask your class to vote on who they think is telling the truth by giving a show of hands. Reveal who the true owner is.
7. Follow Steps 5 and 6 until you have covered all the remaining pictures.

1.20 Most treasured possession

Variation
Ask your students to email you holiday pictures for them to talk about their favourite holiday location.

Talking about something meaningful and cherished will be a key determining factor in the success of the activity.

1.21 My ideal classroom

Focus: Vocabulary of classroom objects

Level: Beginner–Elementary

Time: 10 minutes

ICT skills: Taking digital pictures; uploading, retrieving and pasting the pictures to a page

Preparation:
1. Take a digital picture of your classroom and save it on your computer or pen drive.
2. Open a page on the board and place the picture on it. Enlarge it, to fill the page.

in class

1. Show your students the picture of the classroom that you have taken. Ask them to describe it. Are they happy with their classroom? What changes would they make to it?
2. Invite a student to come up to the board. Select the virtual pen and set the colour to white. Ask the student to rub the pen over anything that he/she is not happy about, covering it in white.
3. Now set the colour of the pen to black. Ask your student to draw into the whitened areas anything that he/she would like to have in the class instead.
4. Tell the student to explain the changes he/she has made in the picture.

Variation 1
Copy and paste the same picture to different pages, allowing several students to participate and making room for comparisons.

Variation 2
Ask your students to send you pictures of their bedroom, and apply the same concept to vocabulary related to house objects.

Variation 3
Ask your students to send you pictures of their own town or neighbourhood.

Everything changes, nothing remains without change. (Gautama Siddharta)

1.22 Out and about

Focus: Functional language for shopping, ordering food and buying tickets

Level: Pre-intermediate–Intermediate

Time: 40 minutes

ICT skills: Finding pictures online; copying and pasting pictures to the board; enlarging objects

Preparation:

1. Browse the web for pictures to illustrate the following conversational shopping situations: buying clothes, ordering food at a fast food restaurant, and buying a ticket for a concert. Choose one picture for each of those situations and copy and paste each to a different page. Enlarge your pictures so they take up most of the space on the page.

2. Write key functional language suitable for the level for each of the shopping situations on the corresponding pages that you would like to introduce or review. Place those expressions below the pictures. Some ideas:
   First page: buying clothes: *Can I help you? It's OK, I'm just looking. Do you think you might have it in red? I'll take it. Your total is ... Here's your change.*
   Second page: ordering food: *Next in line, please. Can I have...? I'll have... Anything else? That's all, thanks.*
   Third page: buying a ticket for a concert: *Do you have any concessions for students? Sitting or standing? Here you are. Thanks a lot. Enjoy the concert.*

in class

1. Tell your students that they are going to spend a day out in London, Melbourne, New York ... (choose a destination that will appeal to them). Tell them that you are going to teletransport them there now; the journey only takes ten seconds, and they will then have a few minutes to form a mental picture of the sounds, the weather, the people and the shops as they walk along the streets, and decide what kinds of things they would like to do there.

2. Count to ten, and allow three or four minutes for the students to visualise. Then elicit from three or four students the mental pictures that they created, and from two or three more what kinds of things they would like to do there.

3. Show the pictures on the board and explain the three situations you have devised for them. Review the vocabulary with them. Ask them for extra key vocabulary that may be added and invite them to write it on the board.

1.22 Out and about

4. Model the conversations with a student, using – among others – the selected phrases.

5. Pair your students so they can talk and practise the key phrases. If you have an odd number of students, pair with one of them. Tell them to reverse roles. Allow enough time for everyone to complete the task before you move on to the following page.

6. Ask at least three pairs to come up to the front and share their dialogues.

7. Ask them open (i.e. not yes/no) questions about the dialogues, such as *What clothes did you buy? How much did you pay for them? Where did you eat? What did you eat? What concert did you see? How much was the ticket?* etc.

Variation
Preparation: show all three situations on one page; scale down the pictures and select a smaller text size for the phrases.
In class: set up three places in the corners of your classroom – a clothes shop, a fast food restaurant and a ticket office – asking students to draw some signs to be displayed in the different corners. Half of your students will be buyers. Divide the remaining half into three even-sized groups to be sellers in the different places. The buyers circulate in the classroom and go from place to place to practise conversations for the corresponding situations. Then reverse roles – buyers become sellers and vice versa.

Coached role-playing activities encourage the students to interact in the target language.

1.23 Picture dominoes

Focus: Establishing connections and associations

Level: Pre-intermediate–Intermediate

Time: 15 minutes

ICT skills: Finding pictures online; copying and pasting pictures to the board; dragging objects on the board

Preparation:
1. Go online and find a wide variety of pictures with no particular connections between them (photos from online newspapers are particularly interesting). Choose around 20 pictures and copy and paste them to a page on the board.

2. Scale down or enlarge the pictures to a similar size, and place them around the four sides of the board.

3. Choose one of your pictures and place it in the middle of the board.

in class
1. Open the document you have created and tell your students that you are going to play a game similar to picture dominoes. Ask your students to look at the pictures on the board and try to find a connection or association between the picture displayed in the middle and any of the pictures around the edge. When a connection or association is found, ask that student to explain it, and then put the two pictures together in the middle.

2. Now ask the students to find any more connections or associations between any of the two pictures placed in the middle and the remaining pictures around the edge, and put the pictures into a pattern over the board, like in a game of dominoes.

3. Conclude the activity when you run out of pictures or your students run out of ideas. Move the pictures back to the sides and play another round, this time with new connections and associations.

Variation
Ask your students each to bring two interesting pictures from a magazine. Provide a large empty area in the classroom by moving the desks to the sides. Ask the students to choose one of their pictures and become a human dominoes piece. Tell them to play dominoes as in the activity above: first, a student stands up in the middle holding his/her picture, then another student places himself/herself next to the first student and explains the

1.23 Picture dominoes

connection, then a third student will place himself/herself next to the first or second student and so on. Play a second round with the remaining pictures.

Creativity is not just the property of exceptional people, but an exceptional property of all people. (Marianne Raynaud)

1.24 Picture idioms

Focus: Reviewing idioms

Level: Intermediate–Advanced

Time: 15 minutes

ICT skills: Dragging objects on the board

Preparation: Select six to ten idiomatic expressions that you would like to review with your class; write each expression on a different page on the board.

in class

1. Open the document you have created and move from page to page, to review with your students the meaning of those idiomatic expressions and think about possible situations where you might use them in conversation.

2. Ask your students to think of something that may have an association with any of the expressions on the board, and then ask a volunteer to come up to the board and draw their idea on the page displaying that particular expression. Encourage maximum participation and make sure that every page has at least one drawing.

3. Now tell your students to look away or close their eyes. Select the virtual pen, set the ink colour to the background colour of the document and run the pen over each of the expressions, thus 'erasing' the text. Leave the drawings untouched.

4. Eyes on the board again. Select one page at random and elicit the idiom from your students. Click on the area where the idiom was written, and drag away your ink blotch to unveil it.

5. Repeat Step 4 with the remaining pages as many times as you wish.

6. Save the document (idioms plus drawings) for future use and revision.

Variation 1
The activity focuses on idioms. However, it may be applied to any other focal vocabulary you would like to review.

Variation 2
Type a story with a strong narrative component to it, such as a fairy tale, or make up a personal story. Break the text up into different fragments and place each fragment on the upper half of a page.

1.24 Picture idioms

Read the story with your students and ask a student up to the board to draw the actions that go along with each fragment, using the space left on the bottom half of the page. Invite a different student each time you open a new page. Then conceal the text with an ink blotch so that your students, led by you as a whole group, retrieve and retell the story by focusing on the drawings. You may also leave two or three key words per line on each page to make it easier for your students. Encourage varied participation and corrections from your students. Finally, use the eraser and remove the ink covering the text on each page for everyone to read the entire story again.

A look at words seen through other people's eyes.

1.25 Picture it

Focus: Present simple tense

Level: Beginner–Elementary

Time: 15 minutes

ICT skills: Taking digital pictures; uploading, retrieving and pasting the pictures to a page

Preparation:
1. Take pictures that can reveal aspects of your life that you would be comfortable sharing; perhaps of your family, friends, your house, your car, a tennis racket, a ticket to a concert, books that you own, etc.
2. Upload the pictures to a pen drive or computer. Paste the pictures to a page.

in class

1. Tell your students that you are going to show them some personal pictures and ask them to think of sentences about your daily life or interests based on the information in the pictures.
2. Show the pictures for your students to call out sentences such as: *Our teacher has two children. He lives in a flat. He has many friends. He drives an old car. He likes playing tennis.* As your students make educated guesses, confirm or deny.
3. Ask for volunteers to write the sentences below the corresponding pictures.
4. You may save the resulting document (pictures and sentences) and print handouts for your students.

Variation 1
Ask some of your students to place their own pictures on a document, and email this to you for the class, thus sharing their own personal experiences.

Variation 2
The same principle can be applied for introducing or reviewing the past simple.

Personal pictures are an invaluable source of meaningful and authentic student-generated material.

1.26 Puzzled!

Focus:	Structuring guesses in English
Level:	Pre-intermediate–Upper Intermediate
Time:	10 minutes
ICT skills:	Finding pictures online; copying and pasting pictures; using the screen capture tool
Preparation:	1. Run a search online for pictures of celebrities (five to ten pictures) your students are likely to recognise.
	2. Copy and paste each of these pictures to a different page.
	3. Open your screen capture application. Break every picture down into fragments with the screen capture application, as if you were creating puzzle pieces, by outlining the area you want to capture with your virtual pen or mouse.
	4. Shuffle the fragments and display them randomly on the page.

in class

1. Tell your students that you have chosen a number of pictures of famous people for them to guess. Introduce key modal verbs or phrases you want them to practise while trying to guess who each of the celebrities is. For example: *may be ...; might be ...; can be ...; could be ...; appears to be ...; looks like ...*

2. Show the puzzle pieces for the first celebrity. Ask someone to drag and place two pieces together, add another one and so on, and let the class guess who that person might be.

Variation
For added fun, include a picture of yourself and one of your students as well.

Motivation is like food for the brain. You cannot get enough in one sitting. It needs continual and regular top ups. (Peter Davies)

CHAPTER 1: IMAGE-BASED ACTIVITIES

1.27 Silent bingo

Focus: Classroom objects

Level: Beginner–Elementary

Time: 15 minutes

ICT skills: Finding pictures online; copying and pasting pictures to a page

Preparation: Go online and look for pictures of 15 to 20 classroom objects. Copy and paste each picture to a page.

in class

1. Show your class the document you have created. Review with them the vocabulary they need to identify each object.

2. Ask your students to take out a piece of paper and draw a table with nine squares in it; this is their bingo card. Then they must write in each of the nine squares the name of a classroom object that they can see on the board (a different word in each square).

3. Click on any picture to prompt the pull-down menu. Click on Cut; the picture will then disappear. If your students have written the name of that object anywhere, they must cross it off their bingo card.

4. Continue cutting the pictures until someone in the class calls Bingo! (In order for anyone to call bingo, all the words on his/her card must have been removed from the board.)

5. Click on your Edit button. Click on Undo to bring back the last picture you cut, and repeat as many times as pictures you have cut to bring back all the pictures again.

6. Tell your students to draw another bingo card, with different objects, to play again. Repeat Steps 3 and 4.

Variation 1
After Step 4, tell your students to draw another table with nine new objects. Then follow Step 5. As your students see a new picture appearing each time, they cross it off from their bingo card if they have it.

Variation 2
Vocabulary review for beginner or elementary students can be carried out for any other target area, e.g. clothes, food and drink, animals, body parts, etc.

Create games that are easy for everyone to follow, to build up strength and self-confidence.

Similar but different

Focus:	Present simple
Level:	Beginner–Elementary
Time:	10 minutes
ICT skills:	Copying and pasting pictures
Preparation:	1. Open a page on your board and draw a line down the middle to divide the page into two. Draw two different faces; one in each half of the page.
	2. Find a selection of pictures online of books, music albums, films, sport equipment, computers and cars. Copy and paste those pictures onto the page with the two faces.
	3. Duplicate some of the pictures (for instance, the book cover or the tennis racket) and place them in both halves. Place the remaining pictures randomly in either half.

in class

1. Elicit from your students what they like doing in their free time. Ask them about what their friends like doing. Tell them to think about a good friend.

2. Pair them, and, ask them to tell each other what things they have in common with that friend and in which ways they are different.

3. Show your class the document you have created. Explain that the two people on the board (James and Steven, for instance) are very good friends. They are similar but different. What do they have in common? Your students should be originating sentences such as: *They both like Harry Potter, They play tennis, James drives a very expensive car but Steven has a very cheap one*, etc.

Variation
Scale down all the pictures and put them together in one corner of the page. Invite a student to come up to the board and read out sentences like the ones above. For each sentence, ask your student to place the pictures in the correct half of the page, restoring them to their original size.

Devise scenarios for constant exposure and repetition, not as a means to practise towards a given end, but as an end in itself.

1.29 Stress patterns

Focus: Showing stress patterns in words

Level: All

Time: 15 minutes

ICT skills: Creating and reproducing objects on the board

Preparation:
1. Create two rectangles of significantly different length and colour. Reproduce the longer rectangle four more times. Reproduce the shorter rectangle seven more times.

2. Place your rectangles on the board this way:

3. This arrangement illustrates the most common word stress patterns in English. Write on the board a selection of words that follow those patterns. The following selection matches the stress patterns above; write these words up on the board in random order:

| teapot | forget | computer | refugee | article |
| actress | machine | important | entertain | telephone |

in class

1. Show your students the document you have created on the board. Explain that each group of rectangles illustrates a different word stress pattern.

2. Ask them to come up to the board in turn and place a word below a stress pattern it fits.

3. Invite your students to add more words that can fit below each pattern.

Variation
Once the activity is finished, you may request your tallest and two other significantly shorter students of about the same height to move up to the front and physically recreate these patterns. Let us say, you are working with the third pattern shown here: the tallest person would stand in the middle with the other two students standing to his/her left and right. Then, as your class calls out the word 'important', for instance, those students raise their arms in synchronicity with the primary and secondary stresses.

Incorporate movement in the classroom, not just as a fun element, but as a required element for certain activities.

Tall – taller – the tallest

Focus: Comparisons in English

Level: Elementary–Pre-intermediate

Time: 15 minutes

ICT skills: Taking digital pictures; uploading, retrieving, pasting and resizing pictures

Preparation:
1. Find pictures online of the basketball players mentioned below.
2. Copy and paste the pictures to a blank page.

in class

1. Show your students the pictures of the following basketball players: Kobe Bryant, Lebron James and Yao Ming. Ask your students if they can recognise those names. Write the corresponding names below the pictures. Ask what the people on the board have in common (they are famous NBA basketball players). Ask what most basketball players tend to have in common (they are usually tall). Highlight the first name and say "Kobe is tall". Highlight the second name and say "Lebron is taller than Kobe". Finally, highlight the third name and say "Yao is the tallest".

2. Invite someone to come up to the board and double-click on any picture and scale it down, thus 'shrinking' the player. Now ask your student to enlarge it, and then invite him/her to make the player look fatter, and finally tell this student to make him look thinner.

3. Place two pictures together. Enlarge the first one vertically, so that the player on it looks significantly taller than the second one. Elicit a sentence from your class, such as: *A is taller than B*.

4. Add a third picture. Make the player on that picture taller than the other two. Elicit a sentence such as *C is the tallest*, or *A is taller than B but not as tall as C*.

5. Encourage your students to come up to the board to play around with the pictures to structure comparisons in English.

Variation
There is a deeper emotional impact if you use students' own pictures on the board. It is a good idea to have a bank of pictures of your students in your computer or pen drive and then you can use those instead of the basketball players.

Try to tap into your students' interests and likes so that they will feel more eager to learn.

The good side / the bad side

Focus: Writing about advantages and disadvantages

Level: Pre-intermediate–Advanced

Time: 10 minutes

ICT skills: Finding pictures online; copying and pasting pictures to a page

Preparation:
1. Find pictures online of the following places: a beach, some mountains, a village and a busy city street.
2. Copy and paste the first two onto one page. Copy and paste the last two to another page. Leave enough room on each page for your students to write sentences.

in class

1. Introduce or review key vocabulary and phrases used for contrasting (for example, *the good side of ... is ... but the bad side of ... is ...; the advantage of ... is ... ; the disadvantage of ... is ... ; however ... ; on the one hand ... but on the other hand ... ;* etc.). Find a couple of scenarios where your students may formulate these contrasts (for example, going to the cinema vs. watching a film at home). Elicit spoken answers.

2. Show the first page of the document you have created (beach vs. mountains). Invite your students to come up to the board and write contrasting sentences.

3. Show the second page (village vs. city life). Invite your students again to come up to the board and write contrasting sentences.

4. Ask your students to think of any other examples of at least two somewhat similar items that could be compared or contrasted. Write them up on the board as they call them out.

5. Set up groups and ask them to discuss the good and bad sides of the items written on the board, using the key vocabulary reviewed.

Variation
Save some of the generated items on the board for your students to write down sentences at home as follow-up work.

'Real' pictures help students form mental pictures, which may help them towards organising information and ideas.

CHAPTER 1: IMAGE-BASED ACTIVITIES

The importance of English

Focus: Reflecting on how important English is for certain jobs

Level: Intermediate–Advanced

Time: 10 minutes

ICT skills: Finding pictures online; copying and pasting pictures to a page

Preparation:
1. Find five to ten pictures online showing different jobs or professionals.
2. Copy and paste those pictures onto a page.

in class

1. You may lead into this activity by asking your students to elaborate on the importance of the English language. How many English-speaking countries can they recall? Can they give you a few examples of English words that have been incorporated into their native language? In addition, ask them for other predominant world languages. What makes them important these days?

2. Show the document you have created. Ask your students to identify the jobs.

3. Invite a student to come up to the board and arrange the pictures according to how important he/she believes English is for the jobs shown in the pictures, explaining his or her decisions.

4. Scramble the pictures, then repeat Step 3 a few more times, with a different student each time. (Scrambling the pictures between each student makes it more likely that they will come up with different answers).

Variation 1
If you had selected ten pictures or more, show only half of them. Scale down the rest to such a degree that your students will not be able to see what is in them. Then gradually pick out those remaining pictures one by one, enlarge them for everyone to see and add them to the ones already showing, prompting a wider variety of answers.

Variation 2
Picture in your mind other topics that can be exploited this way, such as things you would take to a desert island, the most important items at home, the most important things in life. Some topics, such as the most important problems our world faces today, should spark off a lively debate. Depending on the nature of the issue, you could simply write down any necessary words as a replacement to pictures.

Integrate critical thought into your activities to get your students engaged and interested.

1.33 Unfolding story

Focus: Adding details to a story

Level: All

Time: 15 minutes

ICT skills: Finding pictures online; copying and pasting pictures to a page

Preparation:

1. Find five to eight pictures online suitable to be described by your students. For instance, a picture of a busy street, a living room, somebody running away, a building on fire, a social gathering, etc. You may also draw your own pictures on the board.

2. Devise a story around the pictures. (You could first look for the pictures, then think of a plausible story to go along with them. Alternatively, you could think of a story first and then look for pictures that illustrate it.)

3. Open a blank page, and copy and paste the pictures onto it in random order.

in class

1. Tell your students that you are going to share a story with them that you have written.

2. Ask for a volunteer to come up to the front of the class. As you tell the story, he/she drags the pictures into the correct order.

3. Every time the student standing by the board selects a picture, pause the story, and ask your students to describe the picture or scene in it.

4. Once your students have described the picture in question, continue with your story.

5. Repeat Steps 3 and 4 until you have finished the story.

Variation
You may be able to find a sequenced story with text passages and illustrations in your textbook. You could scan the book page and delete –or cover – the text. This could be a motivating way to review or lead into your textbook materials.

Pictures can guide students through a story, and ease understanding of a chain of events.

Weather report

Focus: Expressions related to weather

Level: Elementary–Upper Intermediate

Time: 10 minutes

ICT skills: Finding pictures online; copying and pasting pictures to a page

Preparation:
1. Find a physical map (i.e. featuring mountains, rivers, etc.) online. Copy and paste it onto a page. Enlarge it fully, so that it becomes the background of your page.
2. Draw – or ask someone in your class to draw for you – different objects that symbolise a variety of weather conditions (rain, snow, clouds, etc.). Place the symbols along the bottom of the screen.

in class

1. Show the map, and ask your students, in pairs, to write a very brief imaginary weather report relating to it.
2. Invite a pair of students to come up to the board and, as one student reads their report, the other drags and places the different symbols on the map.
3. Drag the symbols to the bottom of the screen again and invite other pairs to share their report.

Variation 1
Write your own report, and as you read it out somebody in your class places the symbols on the map.

Variation 2
Your students may also use the magnifier tool to focus on certain areas and provide a greater visual impact.

Snowmen fall from heaven ... unassembled.

What's happening?

Focus: Present continuous

Level: Beginner–Elementary

Time: 5 minutes

ICT skills: Searching for pictures online; copying and pasting pictures to a page; spotlight application

Preparation: Find pictures online of a variety of actions; for instance, somebody driving a car or somebody dancing at a party. Paste each action onto its own page.

in class

1. Ask your students to close their eyes for a few seconds. Open the document you have created. Select the spotlight application and reveal only a small area of the picture.

2. Tell your students that they can look at the board now and explain that there is an action hiding on the screen and that you want them to tell you what is happening in the picture. Elicit answers in the present continuous from your students. Move the spotlight over the picture until somebody makes a correct guess. Repeat for each picture you have selected.

Variation 1
The same activity can be adapted for practising past continuous tense (*He was driving a car. She was dancing*; etc.).

Variation 2
Ask your students to email you some pictures they may have, or to find 'action' pictures for this activity.

Grammar seems more stimulating and digestible when presented in a different light.

1.36 What's in there?

Focus: Vocabulary for everyday objects

Level: Beginner–Elementary

Time: 10 minutes

ICT skills: Searching for pictures online; copying and pasting pictures to a page

Preparation:

1. To review, e.g., vocabulary related to rooms of the house, find a picture online of a room such as a kitchen, a bedroom, a bathroom, living room. The more objects you can see in the picture, the better.

2. Copy and paste that picture to a page.

3. Cover that picture with virtual ink the same colour as your background screen, thus creating a visual impression of a blank page.

in class

1. Show your class the document you have created (apparently a blank page). Tell the class that there is a picture hiding. Select the virtual eraser and start erasing anywhere on the board.

2. As you – or a student in the class – erase areas on the board, tell the students to work in pairs and tell each other what is revealed to them (as in *that's a table; that's a chair; that's a shelf;* etc.).

Variation
You can adapt this activity to suit the focal point of your lesson (in a city, at a market, etc.).

There is no such thing as darkness, only a failure to see. (Malcolm Muggeridge)

1.37 Where's Johnny?

Focus: Prepositions of place

Level: Beginner–Elementary

Time: 15–20 minutes

ICT skills: Finding pictures online; copying and pasting pictures; creating objects

Preparation:

1. Find a picture online of a busy city street. Copy and paste the picture to a page.

2. If you have filed any head-and-shoulders photos of your students, retrieve one. Otherwise, draw a small face on the board. Place the photo or drawing somewhere in the street.

3. With your virtual pen, create a small circle filled with red, slightly bigger than the face. Select the circle, click on it and select Duplicate from the pull-down menu. Create 10 to 15 more circles. Place the circles randomly in the street. One of the circles should be covering the face.

in class

1. Show the document you have created. Explain that one of your students is hiding behind one of the red circles and the class will have to try to find him/her. Ask a student to come to the front and hold the digital pen. Elicit questions from your students such as: *Is Johnny on the roof of that building? Is he between the supermarket and the flower shop? Is he by the traffic light? Is he in the middle of the road? Is he on the bus?*, etc. Every time a question has been asked, the red circle is dragged out of the way to reveal – or not – the face.

2. Once the face has been revealed, ask your students to look away or close their eyes for 20 seconds to buy you – or a student – enough time to hide the face behind a different red circle.

3. Repeat Steps 1 and 2 as many times as you wish.

Variation
This activity also deals with vocabulary of street places. So instead of a busy city street, you could use a picture of a room in a house, your classroom, a supermarket, a city map, an office, a park or a market, and then teach and practise the appropriate vocabulary for each of those scenarios.

We learn more by looking for the answer to a question and not finding it than we do from learning the answer itself. (Lloyd Alexander)

Wish you were here

Focus: Describing landscapes

Level: Upper Intermediate–Advanced

Time: 15 minutes

ICT skills: Finding pictures online; copying and pasting pictures to a page

Preparation:

1. Find pictures online of different types of landscape (mountains, beaches, jungles, deserts, lakes etc.); eight pictures is a good number.

2. Copy and paste each picture onto a page on the board. Enlarge the pictures so they take up most of the page space.

3. Provide some key vocabulary for description adequate for the suggested exploitation level with each of the pictures. Annotate the words you want your students to practise on the relevant pages, using a colour that will stand out on the background. For instance, if the picture in particular shows a jungle, you could help them out with words such as *lush vegetation*, *a parrot perched on the branch of a tree* etc.

in class

1. Tell your class that you are going to introduce or review with them vocabulary for landscape descriptions. Introduce a few words that they will be seeing on the board and review them.

2. Divide your students into A and B pairs. Tell them to imagine that they are at an idyllic location. Where would that be? Who would they be with? What would they be doing? What can they see and hear? Ask your students to tell their partner.

3. Now tell your students that you are going to project some idyllic pictures for them to describe. All the B students close their eyes, then you project the first picture for 40 seconds for As to describe to their partner. The As should incorporate into their description the vocabulary provided on the board plus any other vocabulary for the task they can think of.

3. Now it is B's turn; the As close their eyes and the Bs describe the second picture in 40 seconds.

4. Alternate until all eight pictures have been described.

5. Go back to the first picture and reverse the process; the As close their eyes, and the Bs describe it. Then the Bs close their eyes for As to describe the second picture, and so on. But this time

1.38 Wish you were here

remove the vocabulary from the board and challenge your students to try to use the key words that you provided earlier when their partners were describing the first set of pictures.

Variation
After each description of a picture, you may cover it momentarily with the screen curtain application and ask the students listening to the description to draw a picture of it. Then raise the curtain and let your students compare sketches.

For practical ways in which mental imagery can be incorporated into the language classroom, see *Imagine That!* by J. Arnold, H. Puchta and M. Rinvolucri, 2007, Helbling Languages.

Listening with eyes closed may help your students visualise what is being described.

CHAPTER 2
SOUND AND VIDEO-BASED ACTIVITIES

Introduction

Exposing learners regularly to audiovisual material from a wide variety of sources is a pleasant and effective way of bringing language and culture into the classroom. Most coursebooks in the early 21st century are supported by DVDs, and teachers and learners can find an ever-growing number of websites with that type of material. Teachers who use interactive whiteboards connected to the internet agree on the crucial importance of having an internet connection in the classroom.

A board that is connected to the internet allows teachers to further strengthen the interactive nature of lessons that is encouraged in the activities presented in this resource book. Two types of interaction can be envisioned: planned and spontaneous.

In planned interaction, the teacher looks for online material for the class beforehand as part of lesson preparation – bearing in mind that online content may be subject to copyright restrictions – and anticipates student reaction. This material will ideally support, or be supported by, other lesson components and a threefold interaction can then take place: an interaction between the lesson components – which in many instances integrate different sensorial elements – an interaction of the students with the components offered, and an interaction between the students themselves.

For this type of planned or expected interaction the previewed audiovisual material can be accessed in the classroom via an internet connection or via a previous download onto a pen drive or the computer itself. It is normally advisable to save the material, as internet connections may sometimes be down or links may no longer be active; also, saving the material allows its future use.

In many instances, this material can be downloaded without having to use any other program; in other instances, this material is 'streamed', which means it can be watched and/or listened to, but not downloaded unless an additional application is used. There are free applications available online for downloading streamed audio or video material. For sound, *Audacity* is a digital audio editor that, among other features, captures streamed audio. It can be downloaded from http://audacity.sourceforge.net/. For videos, the last basic version of media player *Real Player*, a free download from www.real.com, allows streamed video downloads from most sites (including YouTube). It can also be used to play those videos in flash video format.

Arguably the most exciting kind of interaction for both teachers and students is the spontaneous or unexpected interaction that naturally occurs as part of the teaching/learning experience taking place in the classroom. For this type of interaction, an internet connection in class is required. Suppose that you are welcoming your students to the class and somebody is just putting away his MP3 player. You can ask that student what music he was listening to, and you can then access and play the music videoclip. Then you may ask your students questions based on the video footage or the song lyrics; whether they liked the song or not, what is good or bad about it and so on. Or perhaps you are discussing the topic of food in the classroom and someone mentions that she tried sushi on a recent trip to Rome or

Madrid. Those students who are not familiar with sushi may enjoy watching a short video on how to make it (a search on YouTube for "how to make sushi" should produce some good results). While it is playing, write some key language on the board, then ask your students, in pairs and in turns, to retell each other what they have just learned. Perhaps you have some spare time at the end of a lesson: you can then access the BBC Learning English website and let your students watch a video or listen to a story for five minutes.

In addition to watching and listening, you and your students can hold audio or video conferences with other English speakers outside the classroom as well as making voice recordings or screen recordings, which are useful tools for providing repetition. This work can be posted online or emailed for further language exposure.

These interactions make the learning experience more authentic and realistic, as they extend the language beyond the classroom walls. They are highly motivating and create relevant and meaningful connections. In other words, they are memorable. It is worth pointing out that our minds do not store words in a linear way, as in a dictionary, but in intricate and convoluted ways in which emotions, personal experiences or connections attached to those words are activated when language needs to be retrieved.

Finally, here are some online sites where, at the time of writing, some useful material for the English class can be found:

VIDEO
- www.bbcmotiongallery.com: vast collection of video clip archives
- http://blip.tv: videoblogging site
- www.cnn.com: comprehensive source for news stories
- www.eslvideo.com: video listening exercises for ESL students
- www.jumpcut.com: site for uploading and editing personal videos
- http://sclipo.com: networking site for sharing knowledge through video
- www.teachertube.com: instructional videos for teachers
- www.ted.com: educative talks from inspirational speakers
- www.videojug.com: how-to videos
- www.youtube.com: the most comprehensive video content on the web

AUDIO
- www.bbc.co.uk/worldservice/learningenglish/: a rich menu of varied listening material for learners of English
- www.breakingnewsenglish.com: listening comprehension activities based on current events
- www.britishcouncil.org/learnenglish-central-listening-downloads.htm: listening material for ESL students
- www.elllo.org: over 1,000 listening activities for ESL students
- www.eltpodcast.com: English podcasts for ESL students
- http://en.wikipedia.org/wiki/Wikipedia:Spoken_articles: a

selection of Wikipedia articles in spoken word
- www.esl-lab.com: everyday conversations in English categorised in three language levels
- www.eslpod.com: radio programs for learners of English
- www.vaughanradio.com: radio station for learners of English
- http://voicethread.com: conversations around images and videos

2.1 Audio puzzle

Focus: Understanding listening material; identifying and recalling lines from poems

Level: All

Time: 15–20 minutes

ICT skills: Voice recorder application; creating hyperlinks; dragging objects on the board

Preparation:

1. Find a poem suitable for the age, interests and language level of your class.

2. Open the voice recorder application and record – or ask a student to record – the poem. Record each line or every two lines separately, thus having as many files of recordings as there are lines or pairs of lines.

3. Place the first recording at the top left corner of the board and the last recording at the bottom left corner. Write down or type the content of each short recording next to those two links. Scatter the remaining recordings randomly on the right side of the page

4. Provide handouts of the poem for your students, leaving some gaps for them to fill them in with the corresponding words.

in class

1. Distribute the gapped handouts of the poem.

2. Read out the poem twice for your students to fill in the gaps.

3. Check the answers with your students and address questions from them. Clarify meaning. Invite your students to read out the poem in unison.

4. Next, ask your students to put away their handouts. Show them the page with the hyperlinks on the board. Explain that what they see on the board is an 'audio puzzle', that is, they need to arrange the links in the correct order to reconstruct the poem. The first and last links have already been placed for them.

5. Invite a student to come up to the board and click on any hyperlink and listen to it. It will obviously have to be put somewhere between the two links that have already been located. Ask your student to drag it to what they think the right place is and then write down the content of that recording next to it. Ask the class for confirmation or refusal. Invite other students to come

2.1 Audio puzzle

up to the board to place the remaining links in order and write down the transcripts. As new links and transcripts are being placed in order, it might be necessary to drag the ones already arranged up or down slightly.

6. Once all the links have been arranged, get a student to double-click through the 'pieces of the puzzle' from top to bottom.

Variation 1
Instead of choosing a poem, you may choose a song, a listening passage from your coursebook or a news story from an internet broadcast.

Variation 2
Engage your students in some reading comprehension work. Select a fragment (10 to 15 lines) from the passage. While they are silently reading the text, call the early finishers one at a time to the front to read a couple of different sentences each. Have the microphone and voice recorder ready for them to record their sentences. Then follow the steps for the activity indicated above.

Surprise your students with a listening activity which is not linear but fragmented into pieces.

2.2 Breaking news

Focus: Anticipating relevant focal vocabulary; listening to and understanding authentic news stories

Level: Intermediate–Advanced

Time: 40–60 minutes

ICT skills: Browsing the web and finding clips of short news stories; video player application; hyperlinking web addresses (optional)

Preparation:

1. Find two video clips with short news stories on one of these sites (Sky News, CBS News, CNN News, Yahoo! News) or another site of your choice. Select about 20 key vocabulary items from each of them.

2. Open a page on your board. Create two columns, and as headers copy and paste the web addresses for each of the clips.

3. Write the selected vocabulary on the same page. Jumble up the words from the two stories. Save and file this document.

in class

1. Ask your students if they watch the news on television regularly or if they read newspapers. Do they prefer television, newspapers or the internet? What is news today? Do they know any stories? Can they share them with everyone in class?

2. Open the document and review the words with your students. Explain that the words they see are part of the script of two news stories they will be watching. In groups, your students will put the words into two columns, for the first story or the second one. The students must also produce a logical narrative to anticipate the story.

3. Ask each group or a representative to come up to the board in turn, drag a few of the words into their columns and elaborate on what the group thinks the story is about.

4. Click on the links you have created – or else, open your internet browser and type in the addresses for the clips – and watch the stories.

Variation
You can also choose two news stories from online newspapers or two made-up personal stories as a replacement for the video. Follow Steps 1 and 2 above, but instead of playing video footage, show the written text for the newspaper stories or tell your two stories.

Encourage your students to discern and infer for a more holistic learning experience.

2.3 Bubble story

Focus: Writing dialogues

Level: All

Time: 20 minutes

ICT skills: Video player application; screen capture application; resizing objects; printing handouts from created documents

Preparation:

1. Find a short film scene or a chapter from your coursebook DVD or an EFL DVD that's suitable for your students' language level.

2. Open the video file and the screen capture application.

3. Play the video and pause it each time something interesting or relevant is happening or is about to happen. Using the screen capture application, take pictures of the still frames (10 to 15 pictures is a good number).

4. Resize the pictures and place them in order on a page.

5. Open the virtual pen application and draw some speech bubbles next to the pictures while leaving blank space for your students to write in them.

6. Save the document you have created and print a copy of it.

7. Make an enlarged photocopy or create multiple sheets so that your students have more room to write in the bubbles.

8. Make a copy of the handout for each group of your students.

in class

1. Ask your students if they know what 'bubble stories' are (stories that combine drawings and speech balloons or bubbles, such as comic strips). If so, let someone explain. Otherwise, explain yourself.

2. Distribute the handouts to your students. Explain that the pictures are still frames of a video story they will be watching. Provide some background information on the video.

3. Set up groups and ask your students to fill in the bubbles with dialogue lines. Allow enough time for your students to work in groups, and circulate to help out.

4. Ask your students to pass their stories round to other groups. For example, if you have five groups, Group 1 members pass their

2.3 Bubble story

stories to Group 2, 2 to 3, 3 to 4, 4 to 5, and 5 to 1. Give them enough time to read the stories and note which ones they like best. Then they hand the stories on again in the same way as before.

5. Once all the groups in the class have read all the contributions, they must vote on the best story. Make sure they know that they cannot vote for their own story.

6. Open the document you have created with the captured still frames and the speech bubbles for the group whose members have the best story to write the dialogue lines onto the board.

7. Play the video.

Consider saving the final product, printing handouts and letting your students decorate the classroom with their stories.

2.4 Concentration

Focus:	Reviewing specific vocabulary
Level:	All
Time:	10 minutes
ICT skills:	Using the voice recorder application; creating hyperlinks
Preparation:	1. Select eight key words or phrases you would like to review with your class.
	2. Plug a microphone into your computer and open your voice recorder application. Make 16 short recordings: eight separate recordings for the words or phrases being reviewed and another eight for their definitions (you may use a dictionary or provide your own explanation).
	3. Open a page on your board. Create a colour-filled square with a contrasting border and make 15 copies of it. Lay the 16 squares out in a grid.
	4. Hyperlink each square to one of the recordings you have made.

in class

1. Tell your class that they are going to review some vocabulary learnt recently. Ask them if they have ever heard of the game concentration (or pelmanism). Invite a student who knows the game to explain how to play it, or if necessary explain it yourself.

2. Show the document you have created on the board. Invite one of your students to come up to the board and double-click on any of the squares, prompting a spoken message with either a word/phrase or a definition. Ask him/her to choose another square and double-click on it as well. If the chosen squares form a matching word/definition pair, ask the student to move them away from the grid. Otherwise, they stay there.

3. Continue playing until all the squares have been dragged away from the grid.

4. Shuffle the squares to play more rounds.

Variation 1
Create two sets of squares: one set with English phonemes, e.g. /t/, written in them; the matching set with recordings of either their corresponding sounds or words containing those particular phonemes.

2.4 Concentration

Variation 2
Run an online search for English proverbs or sayings, and choose some you feel will be interesting to your students. Create two sets of squares: one set with the first few words of the proverbs; the matching set with their endings. You could even narrow down your search to a specific word or subject to introduce a new topic in your lesson. Take 'money', for instance. Here are just a few examples: *Money makes ... the world go round. Money doesn't ... grow on trees. Look after the pennies ... and the pounds will look after themselves. Money ... talks. Put your money ... where your mouth is. Money can't buy happiness ... but neither can poverty.*

Variation 3
Choose an even number of students, from 10 to 16. Ask them to come to the front and stand up facing the class. Hand each of those students a card with either a word or its definition which they will have to memorise. Divide the rest of the class into two teams to play the game. The teams will have to call out the names of two students standing, and listen to their words/definitions to see if they are a matching pair. If so, the two standing students go back to their seats. Otherwise, they stay where they are.

Give whatever you are doing and whoever you are with the gift of your attention. (Jim Rohn)

2.5 Controversial issues

Focus: Understanding spoken messages; showing agreement or disagreement on controversial issues, and stating one's opinions

Level: Intermediate–Advanced

Time: 25 minutes

ICT skills: Using the voice recorder application; creating hyperlinks

Preparation:

1. Plug a microphone into your computer and open the voice recording application.

2. Prepare about ten very short statements that you are going to record (each around three to ten seconds long) on controversial issues. For instance, *married people are happier than single people; genetically modified foods are safe; money is the most important thing in the world; smoking shouldn't be allowed anywhere; online dating is dangerous; parents should be permitted to decide the sex of their child; guns should be illegal; no money should be given to beggars; football players are paid too much money; teachers are paid too little money.*

3. Record each of the statements as a separate audio file. Save them in your computer or pen drive.

4. Open a page on your board. Draw a table with the following columns: *agree, disagree, not sure.*

5. Create hyperlinks for each of your recordings. You can number them or choose a word or words that can be associated with the content, e.g. 'smoking', 'parents', 'guns', etc. Place these hyperlinks on the page around the table.

in class

1. Ask a student to come up to the board and double-click on any hyperlink, prompting a spoken controversial statement.

2. Tell your student to drag that hyperlink into one of the columns on the board, depending on his/her feelings on that issue.

3. Ask your other students, in pairs, to discuss whether they agree or disagree with that student's choice. Elicit some diverse opinions.

4. Repeat Steps 1, 2 and 3 until all the audio files have been played. Encourage lively debate.

2.5 Controversial issues

Variation 1
The hyperlink could also incorporate a written version of the audio file to expose your students to that language visually as well as aurally.

Variation 2
Add a dictation exercise to this activity by asking your students to write down what they hear when the hyperlink is double-clicked.

Note
Instead of recording your own voice you could ask somebody else – a native speaker, another teacher or one of your students – to make the recordings for you.

Provide opportunities for class debates and critical thinking.

Disappearing lines

Focus: Key vocabulary for functional language

Level: All

Time: 15 minutes

ICT skills: Video player application; screen capture application

Preparation:

1. Find a video that contains plenty of functional language (for instance, a dialogue between a shop assistant and a customer, or somebody getting street directions). Most DVDs that accompany textbooks, and EFL DVDs, include this type of material.

2. Play the DVD in your computer and open the screen capture application from your board software. Pause the video from time to time and take a picture of the still frame. Take a total of five to ten pictures capturing the language you want to focus on.

3. Place each of the stills on a different page. Write underneath each picture the part of the dialogue corresponding to that particular bit of the story, as shown in the written transcript; alternatively, write something similar that uses the vocabulary you want to focus on in class.

in class

1. Play the video story and follow the lesson outlined in your teacher's book or whatever plan you have decided to follow. Introduce or review the key vocabulary on the captions that you have placed under each still frame.

2. Open the document you have created and ask your students, in pairs, to take roles and read out the dialogues on the board. Move through the pages, giving your students enough time to read out what's written on the screen. Tell your students that they will need to read what they see on the screen loud enough for their partners to hear but not too loud, as it will create too much noise.

3. Go back to page 1. Select the virtual eraser and erase a few words. Ask your students to read out the dialogues again, but this time they will have to recall the words that you erased. Move from page to page, erasing a few words from each page.

4. Repeat Step 3, erasing additional words this time to increase the difficulty level and challenge your students further.

2.6 Disappearing lines

Variation
Draw a conversational scene (shopper and buyer, for example). Copy and paste the drawing onto different pages of the board and write appropriate dialogue lines under each drawing. Follow the instructions above.

Devise engaging contexts to stimulate the acquisition of vocabulary and language chunks.

2.7 DIY karaoke

Focus: Reading song lines

Level: All

Time: 5 minutes

ICT skills: Looking for music video clips and song lyrics online; copying and pasting text; hyperlinking

Preparation:

1. Look for a video clip of a song that you would like to play in class.

2. Now look for the lyrics for that song; run an online search with the song title plus the word 'lyrics'.

3. Hyperlink a page on the board to the video clip.

4. Copy and paste the song lyrics to the same page on the board. Use any available space on the sides to place the lyrics so that they can be easily read.

5. Depending on the kind of the song you are about to play, devise some relevant warm-up work leading to the video clip.

in class

1. Do your warm-up activity.

2. Open the document that you have created. Start playing the song. Select the virtual highlighter and run it – or ask a student to do so – through the words as they are being sung. Your students should be watching the video clip and observing the words being highlighted. Invite everyone to sing along, as if they were at a karaoke party.

Variation 1
Copy and paste the lyrics. Cover them in white ink and gradually reveal them by running the virtual eraser over them as they are sung.

Variation 2
The same concept can be applied to a short video news broadcast. Preview it and type a transcript of it onto the board (make sure it *is* short, as typing a transcript takes a surprisingly long time). In class, play the video for your students to be engaged in both watching the broadcast and reading the transcript.

Songs are excellent examples of authentic language.

2.8 Every film tells a story

Focus: Sequencing; listening to and understanding audiovisual learning materials

Level: All

Time: 30–40 minutes

ICT skills: Browsing the internet for videos, or playing DVDs; printing or emailing handouts from work produced on the board (optional)

Preparation:
1. Choose some video footage with a strong narrative; either finding something on the internet suitable for your class level, or provided by your course teaching materials.
2. Create a list of ten sentences that can summarise the logical chain of events from your video.
3. Open a blank page and write your sentences in a random order.

in class

1. Show your students the document you have created with the misplaced statements. Tell them that they are about to watch a short video but first they need to answer the following questions:
   - By looking at the board, can you predict a title for the story?
   - Can you summarise in a few seconds what the video will be about?
   - Can you reconstruct the story by logically rearranging the sentences on the board?
2. Set up groups and allow time for discussion.
3. Then ask each group or a group representative to come up to the board, rearrange the strips with the sentences and elaborate on the group's choices.
4. Play the video and compare.

Variation
You may also set up other tasks. For example, make up a list with ten selected key words, chunks or phrases from the story. Add to the list five other words, chunks or phrases that are not present in the story. Before watching the video, ask your students to drag away the ones that they think do not belong to the story. Confirm later.
To expand this activity further, distribute monolingual dictionaries and ask each team to be in charge of one word of the ten originally provided. The teams each look for three or four examples of collocations with those words and, as they find them, they write them on the board – but without using the key word.

2.8 Every film tells a story

Once you have a sufficient collection of collocations, invite your students to come up to the board and pair the phrases by dragging key words and collocations together. For extra practice and revision, save this last page with the gapped collocations, and print handouts for your students.

Puzzle your students and pique their curiosity to fully engage them in the activities presented.

2.9 Expanding stories

Focus: Writing narratives; adding details; editing; listening to textbook listening material

Level: All

Time: 30 minutes

ICT skills: Editing text, screen keyboard

Preparation: In your textbook, find a listening comprehension passage with a narrative component that your students have not listened to yet. Open a blank page and type the first two or three lines of the story, using the transcript from the teacher's book.

in class

1. Show your students the beginning of the story. Tell them that you started writing a story for them last night but it got so late and you were so tired that you could barely write three lines.

2. Pique their curiosity by asking questions on what they think the story is about or what is going to happen.

3. Encourage them to volunteer to come up to the board in turns to continue the story using the screen keyboard. They can also use the computer connected to the board. Every contribution should have about two lines.

4. Every time a contribution has been made, ask your students to think of details that they could add to spice the story up. Invite them to make those modifications.

5. If you spot any mistakes, ask your students *Is everything OK?* for necessary adjustments.

6. When the story is complete, engage your students in choral reading and read with them.

7. Tell your class that the story you started writing is actually in their textbooks. Play the listening passage and follow the procedure in the teacher's book or your own lesson plan.

Variation 1
Instead of choosing a listening comprehension passage as the beginning of the story, you could select a reading comprehension text.

2.9 Expanding stories

Variation 2
You can also choose a personal situation, or ask a student to email you an interesting true personal story that they'd like to share. Write its first three lines on the board, and once the class has expanded on them, open the email to see what really happened.

Variation 3
You may also choose a story that you have already seen in class, and challenge your students to reproduce what they read as closely as possible. This is a good opportunity to recycle grammar usage and vocabulary.

Encourage your students to weave stories. They are invaluable platforms for creative use of the language.

2.10 Film dubbers

Focus: Pronunciation, stress and intonation

Level: All

Time: 15 minutes

ICT skills: Video player application; screen recorder application

Preparation:

1. Find a short video with subtitles that you would like to play in class (from your current textbook DVD, an EFL DVD, or a film in English with English subtitles). Ideally, select a scene or a number of scenes with a dialogue (between two, or at most three, people).

2. Import the film to the board with the video player application from the digital board software; make sure that the subtitles are activated.

3. Ensure a microphone is available for the computer you are using, and test it is working.

4. Open the screen recorder application.

in class

1. Explain that you are going to play a short video with sound and subtitles. Tell your students that you want them to focus on pronunciation, stress and intonation; the subtitles will help them understand what is being said. After they watch the video, your students, in pairs or threes – depending on the number of characters in the video – will provide the voices for the film, as you will be turning the sound off. They will still be able to see the subtitles.

2. Play the video with sound and subtitles for your students to watch and listen.

3. Divide your students into their groups and ask them to choose roles. Play the video a second time, with the sound turned off, for the students to read the subtitles on the screen. Remind them they have to keep pace with the subtitles on the screen.

4. Next, tell your groups each to pair with another group, as Group A and Group B. If there is an odd number of groups, pair up with one group. Play the video twice more with the sound turned off, so that Group A can perform for Group B, then vice versa.

5. Invite a group to sit by the computer. Turn the sound off and connect the microphone, for the students to record their voices for the film ('dubbing'). Play the video, and use your screen recorder to record it together with the students' voices.

2.10 Film dubbers

6. Turn the sound on again and play the presentation that your 'film dubbers' have just recorded. Post the video – or part of it if the file is very large – to a blog or website.

Variation 1
Choose a film extract of around one to two minutes in your students' mother tongue. Provide handouts with the transcript, and ask your students, in groups, to translate it into English. Ask your groups to find another group and sit by them. Translations are swapped and the groups do peer editing. The groups get their translations back. Play the film extract, turn the sound off and ask the groups, in turns, to dub the film extract. Select a good group and let them record the dubbing for the film.

Variation 2
The above activity requires advanced digital board competency. However, there is a much simpler, yet still very enjoyable, variation with no recording required: open the video player application, select 'subtitles on' and play the video. Then play the story again, this time with the sound turned off, for your students to dub the film.

Group work maximises students' language practice.

2.11 Hummed greetings

Focus: Stress patterns and intonation in greetings

Level: Beginner

Time: 10 minutes

ICT skills: Voice recorder application; creating hyperlinks; dragging objects on the board

Preparation:

1. Think of a series of greetings you would like to teach or review in class. For instance, *good morning, good afternoon, good evening, good night, hi, hello, see you, see you later, see you tomorrow*.

2. Open the voice recorder application and record the selected greetings one by one as separate files, but instead of reading them out hum them, overemphasising intonation and stress. Save the recordings on your computer or pen drive.

3. Open a page on your board, type the selected greetings, and list them on one side of the board.

4. Hyperlink your recordings to the page and number each of them with a different number. Place those hyperlinks on the other side of the board and randomise their order.

in class

1. Ask your students to tell you greetings they know in English.

2. Open the document you have created with the greetings, and engage your students in choral reading.

3. Bring a student to the front and ask him/her to click on a hyperlink, listen to the hummed greeting and drag it to match its written equivalent.

4. Check with your class whether they agree with the student's choice.

5. Repeat Steps 3 and 4 with other students.

6. Ask your students, in pairs, to hum the greetings on the board for their partners to guess.

Variation 1
Choose any other phrases or full sentences of any nature for higher-level classes, to emphasise the importance of stress and intonation.

2.11 Hummed greetings

Variation 2
Select a brief extract from a reading passage in your textbook (three or four lines will do) and invite your students to hum it. Your students will be focussing on stress and intonation only. These aspects tend to be underestimated, but they are extremely important for developing accurate pronunciation.

To raise an awareness of the subtleties of English pronunciation, have your students concentrate only on the features of stress and intonation, and leave aside word utterance and sound articulation.

2.12 Intonation patterns

Focus: Awareness of intonation patterns in sentences

Level: Pre-intermediate–Intermediate

Time: 15 minutes

ICT skills: Video player application; screen recorder application

Preparation:
1. Find a short video with subtitles that you would like to play in class (from your current coursebook DVD or a film extract, for example).
2. Import the film to the board with the video player application.
3. Open the screen recorder application.
4. Click on the Play button of the video player and the Record button of the screen recorder simultaneously.
5. Select the virtual pen application.
6. Use the upper or lower section of the board to write with the virtual pen the different rising and falling intonation patterns as you notice them on the video soundtrack.
7. Once the video has played through, click on the Record button again to stop the recording.

in class
1. Open the document you have created with the video and the recorded simultaneous annotations to illustrate intonation patterns in English. Play it, pause it, rewind it and comment on the different ways the voice goes up and down in pitch.
2. Play the recording again, this time turning the sound off for your students to follow the subtitles and imitate the intonation patterns while being guided by your annotations.

Variation
Follow Step 2 of the activity. Then open the screen recorder application again and plug a microphone into the computer for your students to record their voices as they read the subtitles with the annotated intonation patterns.

For the general language learner, the pay-offs are greater when sounds are treated within the framework of rhythm and intonation. (Rita Wong, *Teaching Pronunciation*, Prentice Hall, p. 22)

2.13 It's football time

Focus:	Football lexicon
Level:	Intermediate–Advanced
Time:	15 minutes
ICT skills:	Video player application
Preparation:	Find a short video featuring a football game. Review it and think of possible football-related terms that you can introduce in class.

in class

1. Ask your students whether they prefer to watch or to practise sports. Do they like football? How many English teams can they name? How many English international players can they name? (Even if they are not too keen on football, they should at least name David Beckham.) Do they know the word 'soccer'? Where is it used? What does it refer to? ('Soccer' is mainly used in the United States to refer to what the British call 'football'. The word 'football' in the United States refers to 'American football'.)

2. Find out how many football-related words or phrases your students know. Ask a student to come up to the board to write those words and phrases elicited from the other students all around the edges, leaving enough room in the middle to show the video. Introduce any additional words you feel students should know.

3. Open the video file using the video player application in your board software, turn the sound off, and pause it right away.

4. Invite another student to come up to the board and ask him/her to play the video for ten seconds or so and pause it. Then ask him/her to use the virtual highlighter to highlight every word or expression on the board that he/she can associate with the video footage played so far. He or she will also have to say a sentence with the word or words in question. For instance: *Player number ten got fouled. The stands are packed. The referee showed a yellow card. Number 8 was offside.*

5. Repeat Step 4 a few more times with other students. You may remove some of the words on the board and replace them with other key vocabulary.

Variation
Record a very short video with your digital camera as you are walking around in the city. Elicit city street vocabulary before you play the video in class.
Think of any other locations and focal vocabulary for them.

Provide opportunities for student-generated content.

2.14 Jumbled-up song lines

Focus: Word order in song lines

Level: All

Time: 20 minutes

ICT skills: Dragging objects on the board

Preparation:

1. Find a song whose lyrics are suitable for your students' language level. Make sure there are enough lines of verse to have at least one line for every three students in your class.

2. Print a copy of the song lyrics.

3. Open a page on the board and write the words of the first line of the song as separate items or objects, so that they can be independently dragged. Jumble the words up and place them randomly on the page.

4. Open another page and follow Step 3, this time with the words of the second line of the song. Follow the same procedure for the remaining lines.

5. Devise some warm-up work that fits the song you have chosen.

in class

1. Do your warm-up activity.

2. Set up groups of three to five students. Show the first page on the board. Ask the first group to come up and drag the words to form the first song line. Let the students deliberate for a minute or two. If they are right in their prediction, award them two points. If their prediction is incorrect, start playing the song and pause immediately after the last word in that line. Again, let them deliberate, and put the words into the right order. If they get it right this time, award one point. If it is still incorrect, no points are awarded, and the next team comes up and has a go, for the chance to win one point. If they too are incorrect, the following team has a go, and so on.

3. Move to the next page of the document and invite the next group to work out the second line. Do the same for each of the remaining groups.

4. When all the words in every line have been placed in the right order, play the song again, moving forward from page to page and encouraging your students to sing along.

2.14 Jumbled-up song lines

Variation
Follow the same procedure but use a poem this time instead of a song.

A pleasant way to work on grammatical patterns, word order and collocations.

2.15 Karaoke makers

Focus: Recognising and sequencing song lyrics

Level: All

Time: 35 minutes

ICT skills: Dragging objects on the board; video player application; screen recorder application

Preparation:
1. Find a video clip of a song suited to your students' language level.

2. Print a copy of the song lyrics. Make enough enlarged copies of the song for your students; if you are going to divide the class into five groups, make five copies. Cut the copies into strips, one strip per line of song.

3. Open the video player application and place the video file on a page. Write the song lines, in random order, on the right-hand side of the board.

in class

1. Write up the following questions on the board for your students to discuss in groups:
   a) Does the word *karaoke* come from English, Spanish or Japanese? (**Key**: from Japanese *kara*, meaning 'empty', and *okesutora*, meaning 'orchestra').
   b) Have you ever been to a karaoke bar or karaoke party? Did you sing?
   c) If we had a karaoke party here now, which English song would you like to sing? Can you sing a line or two?

2. Once your students have discussed those questions, elicit answers for students to share with all the groups.

3. Give each group a set of the jumbled-up lyrics in strips, which should be distributed amongst the group members. Tell your groups to make a space to place the strips one below each other, as they hear the matching lyrics once you start playing the song.

4. Play the song, so that your students can place the strips in order. Play the song again for confirmation or to give groups that may need more time a better chance to arrange the strips.

5. Invite a student to come up to the board and drag the song lines into the correct order, reproducing the way the group pieced the strips together.

2.15 Karaoke makers

6. Now ask a couple of students to come up to the board; one of them drags a song line on the board to the bottom of the video screen just as he/she hears it sung, then moves it out of the way to the left-hand side of the board. The other student can then drag the next song line to the bottom of the screen, move it out of the way and so they take turns to move the lyrics, as in a karaoke video clip.

7. Open the screen recorder application, play the video clip and record the students performing Step 6.

8. Retrieve the recording that you made. Invite all your students to watch the video clip with the karaoke captions and sing along with it.

Variation
Find a short recording with a strong narrative component to it. Mute the sound and create strips of paper describing the actions on the video. Follow the same procedure as shown above.

Note
A good resource for you and your students to find information on the topic of karaoke is: http://en.wikipedia.org/wiki/Karaoke. You can also find many karaoke versions of popular songs by accessing www.youtube.com and typing "videoke" into the search box. Another excellent resource for an online karaoke party is www.karaokeparty.com.

A good way to develop positive group feeling.

2.16 Moody sounds

Focus: Identifying moods

Level: Intermediate

Time: 15 minutes

ICT skills: Voice recorder application; creating hyperlinks

Preparation:

1. Plug a microphone into your computer and open a voice recording application.

2. Think of two statements that can be expressed in different ways according to the mood you happen to be in, for example: *I'm leaving tomorrow.* Record one of the statements in a variety of ways indicating different moods: angry, relieved, happy, sad, excited, surprised, furious etc. Each mood should have a separate recording. Save the recordings on your computer or pen drive.

3. Open a page on your board. Draw a table with as many columns as mood recordings you have made. Head each column with the word for the mood.

4. Create hyperlinks for each of your recordings. Number each of the hyperlinks and place them outside the chart area.

5. Write the second statement on a separate page.

in class

1. Tell your class that they are going to hear several recordings of a spoken statement. Each recording indicates a different mood, and they have to identify those moods.

2. Open the document you have created. Ask your students to listen to the recordings, and write down the number of each recording and the mood on the board they would match it to.

3. Once you have played all the recordings, invite one of your students to come up to the board and drag the numbered links into their corresponding columns. Ask the class if they agree with the student's answers.

4. Review all the moods with your class again and encourage choral reading to show the mood.

5. Open the page with the second statement, and invite your students to choral read it in ways to match the moods.

2.16 Moody sounds

Variation
Prompt from your students any other moods not written on the board, and ask them to speak the statements showing those moods.

Work in the sound system now emphasises the importance of the suprasegmental features (i.e. stress, rhythm and intonation) and their use not just to complement meaning but to create meaning.
(Joan Morley, 'Trends in Speech/Pronunciation Instructional Theory and Practice', *TESOL Matters*, August/Sept. 1999)

2.17 Odd words

Focus:	Discriminating sounds
Level:	All
Time:	15 minutes
ICT skills:	Dragging objects on the board
Preparation:	1. Find a song that you would like to play in class.
	2. Take a close look at the lyrics; select key vocabulary from the song (about four or five verbs, four or five adjectives and four or five nouns).
	3. Write down the words you have selected in random order on the board. Add between them another five or six verbs, adjectives and nouns not present in the song, but more or less similar in meaning.

in class

1. Open the document you have created on the board. Explain that most of the words written on the board have been taken from the song they are about to listen to. Ask your students to get into groups of four or five and, using the words on the board, think of a possible title for the song. Your students, in groups, can also make guesses about the possible meaning of the lyrics, then share their guesses with the class.

2. Play the song. As they listen to it, it is your students' task to decide which words on the board do not belong to the song.

3. Ask a student in your class to come up to the front and drag to one corner of the board the words that were not part of the song lyrics.

4. Confirm this with the rest of your students. Invite anyone to alter the student's choices.

5. Repeat Step 4 if there are still any changes to be made.

6. Play the song again.

Variation
Use phonetically transcribed words instead of spelled-out ones.

Invite students to use the language in creative ways.

Reporting verbs

Focus: Reporting verbs in reported speech

Level: Intermediate–Advanced

Time: 20 minutes

ICT skills: Video player application

Preparation:

1. Run an online search for a short video – or an extract of a longer video – featuring an interview. Copy and paste the link to the video.

2. Open the video application on the board. Preview the video. Use the space left around the video screen to write common reporting verbs that you would like to introduce or review in your class, for example: *say, tell, ask, agree, announce, apologise, complain, deny, explain, promise, refuse, suggest, warn* – making sure you include many that are in the video.

in class

1. Open the document you have created and review the reporting verbs on the board. Emphasise the direct and reported speech grammar patterns they require. Devise situations in which those reporting verbs would be used.

2. Tell your students that you are going to play a video with an interview. Play the whole length of the video without pausing.

3. Invite a student to come up to the board. Ask the student to play the video again and pause whenever he/she can report something being said with a reporting verb displayed on the screen. He/she should pause the video, select the virtual highlighter, highlight the verb and produce a reporting sentence with that verb.

4. Repeat Step 3 several times, inviting a different student each time.

5. Ask the class to write up an account of the interview using a variety of reporting verbs.

Variation 1
Use a film scene with a dialogue.

Variation 2
Pause the video yourself, highlight a verb and ask your students to produce a sentence with the reporting verb.

Let your students decide on a popular English speaker of their choice and find the video material you need by running this search on www.youtube.com: "name of person+interview".

2.19 Silent film

Focus: Describing actions

Level: Intermediate

Time: 10 minutes

ICT skills: None

Preparation: Find a short video story with plenty of action (an extract from an action film or, better still, a silent film, works perfectly for this activity).

in class

1. Tell your students to close their eyes. They are about to take turns to tell a story which will be based on the video you will be showing on the screen. Tell them they can only open their eyes if tapped on their shoulder, and when tapped a second time they must close their eyes again. Give them some background information on the video footage that you are about to play.

2. If you are not playing a silent film, open your video player application and turn the sound off.

3. Students' eyes closed. Start playing the film and tap someone on the shoulder, then go back to the front in order to pause the film when you think your student needs more time to say what he/she is seeing.

4. Tap this student a second time so he/she closes his/her eyes again, and tap another student in turn, to watch and tell.

5. Repeat with other students in the class until you reach the end of the film.

6. Students open their eyes; play the film again for your students to watch from beginning to end.

Extension
7. Set up small groups and ask each group to prepare a short scene as if for a silent film. Invite them to perform to the class and, as they do so, the students in the other groups close their eyes and take turns, as indicated above, to describe what they are seeing.

A friendly and productive learning environment increases students' confidence.

Snakes and Ladders online news

Focus: Video-based comprehension questions

Level: Upper Intermediate–Advanced

Time: 40 minutes

ICT skills: Finding videos online; drawing a grid; creating objects and dragging them; hyperlinking video clips; virtual dice application

Preparation:

1. Draw on the board a replica of the board game Snakes and Ladders. Alternatively, search for a picture of it online and copy, paste and enlarge the picture on the board.

2. Go online and find 8 to 12 news stories on video. CNN News, (www.cnn.com) offers a rich variety of short news stories on video that are ideal for this level. The videos usually range from two to four minutes in length – do not select any that are longer than this.

3. Hyperlink the selected videos to an equal number of squares of your choice on the board. Across the top of the board, write *The Five Ws –Who? What? Where? When? Why?*

4. Create circles of different colours to use as counters for the game; the size of each circle should be about half the size of a grid square.

5. Bring a real die to class if you're not using virtual dice.

in class

1. Tell your students that they are about to play a board game. Can they name any board names? (They may mention games such as Pictionary, Scrabble, Taboo, Parchisi, Scattergories or Monopoly). What are the rules involved for the games they mentioned? Ask them if they know the game Snakes and Ladders. Open the document you have created, to illustrate and provide any explanations necessary for them to understand how to play.

2. Set up four or five groups in your class and invite the whole class in groups to play the game; that is, each group will be playing as one player. Explain that some squares have news stories linked to them, and when a group lands on any of those squares, they will watch the video story, and then they must answer the five Ws about the news story on that square. Depending on the particular story, some of the Ws may not be obvious, but invite them to make something up for each of them. Assure them that, as the judge of the competition, you will be fair in accepting or rejecting

Snakes and Ladders online news

their answers. For an acceptable answer on each of the questions, they get one point (so a maximum of 5 points can be gained by landing on one of the selected squares).

3. Select the virtual dice application in your software or, alternatively, use a real die. Start the game; you or a student may move the 'counters'. If a group lands on a video-linked square that has already been landed on, they roll the die again.

4. The winning group will be the one with the highest number of points after everyone has reached the end square.

Variation
Instead of using video news stories, you may also use streaming or recorded audio material.

Talent wins games, but teamwork and intelligence wins championships. (Michael Jordan)

Sounds familiar

Focus: Personal descriptions; family members

Level: Beginner–Elementary

Time: 15 minutes

ICT skills: Voice recorder application; hyperlinking files

Preparation:

1. Prepare four short passages describing the members of an imaginary family, for example, a mother, a father, a daughter and a son. You may include a brief physical description of each, their ages, their likes and how they relate to each other.

2. Open the voice recorder application in your computer and record those four passages as separate files.

3. Open a page on your board and draw a sketch of each the four people. Make sure your drawings match the descriptions you have recorded.

4. Write the name of each family member next to the drawing of him or her, and hyperlink those names to the audio files that you recorded.

in class

1. Go around the room and give each student a letter: A, B, C, D. Explain that, according to the letter they have, they will have to take notes on a family member (for instance, As are the mother, Bs the father, etc. Open the document you have created, ask your students to get pen and paper for a dictation and tell them to take notes only on the family member they have been assigned. Explain that they probably won't have enough time to be able to write down everything they hear, but they should try to gather as much information as possible.

2. Click on the names on the board and play the audio files one by one twice. Your students should be taking notes.

3. Ask all As, Bs, Cs and Ds to meet in groups; three or four same-letter students per group.

4. The students cooperate in groups, to try to produce a full written transcript of the recording.

5. Invite your students to come up to the board and write down their transcript.

6. Play the audio files again and compare.

CHAPTER 2: SOUND AND VIDEO-BASED ACTIVITIES 111

2.21 Sounds familiar

Variation 1
Use photos of real family members instead of drawings.

Variation 2
Ask your students to email an attached personal recording with descriptions of their family that they and their family are happy to share. Play the recordings in class and bring students up to the front to draw the family members as they listen to the recording.

Decoding the sounds of English and recoding them in writing is a major learning task.
(Paul Davis and Mario Rinvolucri, *Dictation: New Methods, New Possibilities*, Cambridge University Press, 1988)

Still frames

Focus: Sequencing events; creating a story around pictures

Level: Pre-intermediate–Advanced

Time: 20 minutes

ICT skills: Video player application; screen capture application

Preparation:

1. Find a short video story, or a unit from your coursebook DVD or an EFL DVD, with a strong narrative component.

2. Open the video application and the screen capture application. Start playing the video, and pause it when something interesting or relevant happens or is about to happen. Take a picture of the still frame with the screen capture application. Repeat this action eight to ten times. Place the pictures of these still frames on a single page.

3. Compose some comprehension questions relating to the video.

in class

1. Show your class the page with the still frames. Tell them that those pictures are part of a video story they will be watching. Provide some background information about the story, and some key vocabulary.

2. Set up groups to write a short story based on the pictures on the board; five to eight lines should be long enough. Their story does not need to be the same as the one on the video. Circulate to provide any help they may need. Allow enough time for your students to write up the story.

3. Your groups read out their stories. Provide feedback. Ask the class which story they liked the best.

4. Finally, play the video.

5. Ask your comprehension questions on the video.

Variation 1
For extra creativity, jumble up the pictures on the page so they are in an order different from the one in which they appear on the video.

Variation 2
Ask your students to write dialogues instead of a narrative account.

Variation 3
Decorate the classroom walls with the students' stories.

Cooperative learning promotes self-esteem amongst students.

2.23 Talking categories

Focus: Vocabulary recall

Level: Pre-intermediate–Intermediate

Time: 20 minutes

ICT skills: Voice recorder application; creating hyperlinks

Preparation:
1. Think of a series of words of phrases that can be used to categorise nouns, either abstract or concrete. Here is a list suitable for this level: *lives in water; works on electricity; bigger than an elephant; circular; square; smaller than a coin; is red; is used at home; found in the country; can be read; a drink; smells bad; it's hot; it melts; song title.*

2. Open the voice recording application in your computer and record each of the categories suggested above (or your own) as separate files. Save them in your computer or pen drive.

3. Open a page on the board and hyperlink all your recordings to it. Assign a number to each of the recordings.

in class

1. Set up groups of four to five students. Explain that they are going to play a game based on categorising words. Show the document you have created on the board. Tell your students that each time a numbered box is double-clicked, a very short audio file will be heard, providing one category. In groups, they will have to think of as many nouns as possible that can be categorised that way, starting with a letter you will be giving them. They have one minute per round.

2. Ask a student to choose a number from the board to click on. Let us say, the chosen number is 3 and, as you click on it, the spoken message that results is *bigger than an elephant*. Then tell a student to call out 'Stop!' any time they want to in the next minute or so, and start reciting the alphabet to yourself. When they do so, write down the letter you happened to be reciting right then. If it was M, the groups have one minute to write down, on one piece of paper per group, as many words as they can starting with M under the category of 'bigger than an elephant' (*museum; Morocco; mountain; motorway;* etc.).

3. When time is up, collect the papers from your students, and read out the words they thought of, counting the number of correct answers; the group with the greatest number wins.

Talking categories

4. Ask another student to call out a different number on the board. Repeat Steps 2 and 3 for each category.

Variation 1
Collect and save all the pieces of paper. A week or two later, list some of the answers on the board but not the categories themselves (for instance, *museum*; *Morocco*; *mountain*; *motorway*...) for your students to suggest possible category tags (which may not necessarily be the ones you provided in the original activity but could be equally valid).

Variation 2
Instead of audio links you could use written categories – but the audio component brings an added element of interactivity and excitement.

An effective game for vocabulary retrieval.

2.24 The newsroom

Focus: Predicting information; generating questions; watching and understanding news stories

Level: Intermediate–Advanced

Time: 40 minutes

ICT skills: Finding pictures online; copying and pasting pictures to a page; browsing the web and finding clips of short news stories (suggested web sites: Sky News, BBC News, CBS News, CNN News, Yahoo News); hyperlinking web addresses (optional)

Preparation:

1. Browse internet editions of newspapers for one or two current news stories likely to be of interest to your students. Find pictures attached to the articles. Copy and paste the picture or pictures to a page.

2. Run a search for the same stories on video on the suggested sites or a different site of your choice. Copy and paste the embedded address or addresses into the document you have created. Alternatively, hyperlink the pictures to the video clips.

3. This process may be reversed, that is, first find the video footage, then look for the written article with the pictures.

in class

1. Ask your class if they are keeping up to date with the latest news. What is the news today? Do they know any online news services in English? (They may mention CNN, BBC, *New York Times*, *The Times*). Ask someone to access the sites and have a look at the home pages.

2. Tell your students you have selected one or two news stories for them to watch in class. Show the picture(s) and invite the students to describe them and make predictions about what they refer to. For instance, what has just happened? or what is going to happen?

3. Ask your students to come up to the board and write under each of the pictures relevant questions that may be addressed on the news broadcast you will be playing later. If too many questions are generated, negotiate with the class how many they want to keep or which ones they think could be more interesting or more likely to generate an answer. Ask them to write those questions on a sheet of paper.

2.24 The newsroom

4. Invite your students to watch the broadcast and take notes on the answers to their questions if applicable. Click on the links you have created, or open your internet browser and type in the addresses for the clips – and watch the stories.

Extension
5. Erase the questions under the pictures, and write a sentence relevant to each one. Ask your students to come up to the board and start expanding the stories with the information gathered from the video clip, until they have filled the space available at the bottom.

Variation 1
Additionally, you may ask your students to write a report in class or at home, based on the information gathered.

Let students be creatively involved in generating their own questions for the language materials.

2.25 Video auction

Focus: Predicting words

Level: Upper Intermediate–Advanced

Time: 30–40 minutes

ICT skills: Dragging objects on the board

Preparation:
1. Find a short film scene – preferably with subtitles – with a dialogue that you would like to play in class. Ideally the scene should have around 15 utterances.

2. Transcribe the film dialogue.

3. Open the video player application from your board software. Do not play the video yet.

4. On one side of the video screen, type the lines from the dialogue in a list, leaving a gap for the last word in each line. For instance, if the line in question is *May the force be with you,* type *May the force be with …* . Number each line.

5. Create a colour-filled rectangle big enough to cover all the lines, and place the rectangle over them.

in class

1. Introduce the term 'auction'. Ask your students what kinds of goods are sold at auctions. Have they ever bid for anything at an auction? Ask them if they have heard of eBay auctions. Have they ever bought or sold anything on eBay? You may access the eBay site for your students to see (www.ebay.com).

2. Tell your students that they are going to participate in a film auction. Explain that, in groups, they are going to guess, and write down, the last word of each line in the film scene that you are going to play, and then bid for the line. You will reveal the first line before you start playing the film.

3. Each group will have $1,000 to spend. They can bid as much money as they want for each of the lines, but they must not reveal their answer – the missing word – while they are bidding for it. The highest bidder will win the line if the word they have guessed is the same as the missing word. But if they are wrong, the second highest bidder gets a chance to win it, and so on. The group winning the line has the amount they have bid subtracted from their total money. The aim of the video auction is for each group to buy as many lines as possible with the $1,000.

2.25 Video auction

4. Start the auction: set up groups of three to five. Drag the rectangle down just enough to reveal the first line. Give the students a minute or two to guess the missing word, and for each group to write down the one they decide on. Then start the bidding. Once the bidding for that line is complete, play the film and pause it right after the missing word comes up, then check what the top bidders have written, to determine who has won the line.

5. Repeat this procedure for all of the lines.

Extension
6. Ask your students to brainstorm famous film quotes. Here are some very famous ones:
"ET phone home." (ET); "Frankly, my dear, I don't give a damn." (Gone With the Wind); "Bond. James Bond." (James Bond films); "Life is like a box of chocolates; you never know what you're gonna get." (Forrest Gump).

Variation 1
Use a song instead of video footage.

Variation 2
Provide scrambled words for each line, and ask your students to put them into the correct order.

A formula guaranteed to build up interest and foster concentration in listening practice.

2.26 Videoclip quiz

Focus: General vocabulary review

Level: All

Time: 20 minutes

ICT skills: Finding a music video clip online; creating and dragging objects on the board

Preparation:
1. Find a music video clip appropriate for your class's age, interests and language level.

2. Open your video player application and use the space available on the left and right hand side of the screen to type up two sets of questions. On one side write the heading 'Video' and type up a set of five to ten questions based on the video footage, such as *Was the man carrying an umbrella or a suitcase?; Did the man walk into a bar or a shop?; What was the colour of the car he was driving?;* etc. On the other side, write the heading 'Lyrics' and type up a set of five to ten questions based on the song lyrics; you could create multiple choice questions for words missing from the song lines, such as (for the song *Yesterday*): *Yesterday, all my troubles .... so far away*: with possible answers: a) are   b) seemed   c) were   d) went.

3. Create two colour-filled rectangles big enough to cover the two sets of questions. Cover the two sides of the board with the rectangles.

4. Depending on the kind of the song you are about to play, devise some relevant warm-up work leading to the video clip.

in class

1. Do your warm-up activity.

2. Open the document you have created and play the video clip.

3. Set up groups of three to five students and tell them about the two sets of questions. Establish an order for the groups to answer the questions. Each group may choose a question based on either the video or the song lyrics. A correct answer gives them one point. If their answer is incorrect, the next team tries to answer, for one point. If this second team fails to provide a correct answer, the next team in order tries, until the correct answer is given.

2.26 Videoclip quiz

4. Start the game. Gradually drag the rectangles down to reveal the questions as the game is played.

Variation
For the lyrics, instead of providing multiple choice answers, simply leave gaps for your students to think of the correct word.

Sink or swim together!

2.27 Whose line is it?

Focus:	Encouraging oral fluency; listening to authentic material; writing dialogues
Level:	Intermediate–Advanced
Time:	50 minutes
ICT skills:	Searching for films online; dragging objects on the board; hyperlinking websites (optional)

Preparation:

1. Find a film trailer online for a current or upcoming film release that will be of interest to your students and appropriate to their age and interests. Try the search term "film trailers" or "movie trailers".

2. Hyperlink the site to a blank document, or note the address to type into your web browser in class.

3. Preview the trailer and select a variety of key lines from dialogues in it (10 to 15 is a good number). Open a blank page and write them down, in random order.

in class

1. Ask your students about the last time they went to the cinema. Which film did they watch? Was it good? What is the best film they have ever seen? Do they know the films being screened right now?

2. Tell the class that they are going to preview a current film but before that, you are going to set up groups and they will have to prepare short sketches based on the film.

3. Show them the key lines on the board. Explain that this is just a selection of actual lines from dialogues in the film, although not in the right order. Go over the lines to clarify meaning.

4. Ask them if anybody knows the film that you have chosen for them. If so, ask them to say what they know about it, briefly outlining the plot, characters, location, etc.

5. In groups, they must create a short sketch – one to two minutes – using as many as they wish of the lines they can see on the board, in any order, and adding some more lines of their own choice. It is up to them to decide how many characters their trailer will have, and whether they are going to have special effects, a narrator, etc. It is not imperative that everyone in the group should perform in front of the class; however, they all must make contributions while preparing the sketch. Ask them not to bring any notes with them while they are performing.

2.27 Whose line is it?

6. Allow about 10 minutes for them to prepare the sketches and rehearse.

7. In turns, the groups come to the front and explain their story. Then on the board they drag the lines they will be using into the right order for their sketch, and drag away the ones they are not using. Then they perform their sketch.

8. After all the groups have performed, watch the trailer on your big screen.

Extension

9. Hold an awards ceremony. The students can vote for 'best actor', 'best actress', 'best sketch', 'best special effects', 'best plot', 'best pronunciation', etc.

10. As the winners are announced, they can improvise a short 'thank you' speech (which would give you an excellent opportunity to introduce key vocabulary such *as I am honoured to receive ... I would like to acknowledge ...* etc.

Empower your students with inspiring student-centred activities.

CHAPTER 3
TEXT-BASED ACTIVITIES

Introduction

Although interactive whiteboards combine many distinct features that are extremely effective in the classroom setting, the most usual action performed on them is displaying text. However, as far as displaying text is concerned, they present clear benefits over traditional boards. Text can not only be handwritten with the virtual pen or in some instances with a finger, but generated in advance. The most evident advantage here is the visual aspect of the text displayed; it can be resized, and different colours and fonts can be combined. Pages containing text can be flicked through or scrolled down without the need to erase to make room for more. There is no need to erase and rewrite text for a new class, as it can be saved, retrieved and used again. It can also be placed on the board by being copied and pasted from a particular source or shown from a document or the internet. It can also be input directly by you and students, and for that purpose the accompanying software provides handwriting recognition tools and screen keyboards, and the computer keyboard itself may be used as well.

The overall benefits for the language classroom of this versatile nature of interactive whiteboards are really thrilling. Users are able to manipulate text in a tactile way such as by dragging and dropping text on the board. This is particularly helpful when you want to create activities based on matching words and meanings, or arranging scrambled paragraphs into a logical order, labelling objects, choosing headlines or sequencing events, among others. Gapped text activities which can provide practice in vocabulary and text cohesion and coherence can also be created in many different ways, such as by placing the text and then covering the words you want to be missing with a pen the same colour as the background; to reveal the words, simply use the eraser tool to rub off the 'ink' and reveal the hidden words. You may also place colour-filled rectangles over certain words and then remove them by dragging them. In addition, there are many other more sophisticated and more visually impressive techniques for hiding and revealing text ready for you to explore.

Another aspect of interactive whiteboards that is especially relevant to language teachers is the ability to project student work that may have been published in a blog, or emailed, or stored in a pen drive. Even work that is actually being produced in the classroom can be scanned or photographed, uploaded to the computer and projected. Then suggestions and feedback can be made on the board. Text-based material that may have been saved with word processors or applications such as PowerPoint can equally well be retrieved, projected and enriched with further annotations or links to multimedia supporting information.

The internet of course provides up-to-date reading material which can be of interest and relevance to the English language class. Text from the internet can be copied and pasted and then quickly and easily modified by simplifying some words or expressions, or shortening them, to accommodate your students' language level. An ever-growing wealth of online newspapers, encyclopedias and dictionaries – the latter often providing audible pronunciation – can assist the teacher and students in the classroom setting wherever help is needed or curiosity is aroused.

There is an increasing tendency nowadays among publishers to provide digital versions of their coursebooks. This means that all the different course components can be accessed via the board: text itself and also audio and video material, games, picture banks and supplementary activities. This allows the teacher to focus the attention of the class onto both his or her own activities and to what is being shown on the board while working with the textbook.

And finally, the students can come up to the board and interact with the teaching material in many inviting ways, their enjoyable experience leading to the formation of strong and lasting memories.

3.1 Avid readers

Focus: Review of words and expressions used to give views on books and reading preferences

Level: Upper Intermediate–Advanced

Time: 20-30 minutes

ICT skills: None

Preparation:

1. Think of key words and expressions used to give views on books. Your students will have been exposed to these words and expressions previously in class, and so will be familiar with them. The selected vocabulary should be specific to their language level (possible examples: *an avid reader; bookworm; to be keen on; can't put a book down; worth reading; a thought-provoking story; a gripping plot;* etc).

2. Open a blank page on your board. Write down the vocabulary.

in class

1. Tell your students that they are going to review some key vocabulary used to give views on books. Open the document with the phrases that you have written.

2. Invite your students to come up to the board and write possible conversational questions using the expressions on the board. For example, using 'avid reader' they could ask questions such as *Are you an avid reader? Do you know any avid readers in this class? Do you think the teacher is an avid reader?* and so on. Make a list of 10 to 15 questions.

3. Create a space in your classroom and ask your students to stand up and make two circles, the inner one with the students facing outwards and the outer circle with the students facing towards the centre. Each circle needs an equal number of members, so if you have an odd number of students, join in.

4. Tell the students that you will give them a question to ask a partner, as if for an interview, and that after they have heard the reply they will need to think of a follow-up question themselves and again listen to the reply. Make sure that your students understand that they all have to move at the same pace, following your cues.

CHAPTER 3: TEXT-BASED ACTIVITIES

3.1 Avid readers

5. Then read out the first question on the board. Each student in the outer circle asks it to their partner in the inner circle, and after hearing the answer, asks their follow-up question and hears the answer. Allow time for the interviews to be completed. Then tell everyone in the outer circle to move one spot to the right, thus facing somebody else. This time, the people in the inner circle will be asking the questions. Follow this procedure until all the questions on the board have been covered.

Variation 1
Encourage your students to send you emails after class with answers to some of those questions, making sure they know that what they write will be seen by the class. Open them and share them next time you see your students in class.

Variation 2
Any topic contained in your syllabus can be reviewed this way. Reading is just one example of the many possibilities.

Recognise diversity and different learning styles, and make provision for kinaesthetic learners.

From rags to riches

Focus: Expressions used to talk about having or lacking money

Level: Intermediate–Advanced

Time: 15 minutes

ICT skills: Dragging objects on the board

Preparation: List the following expressions, related to money, on your board: *to be made of money, to be in the red, to be loaded, to be bankrupt, to be strapped for cash, to be well off, to be broke, to make ends meet.*

in class

1. Introduce the activity by asking your students if they have ever heard the expression 'from rags to riches' (also 'and back again'). Elicit the explanation from your students, or explain it yourself. Ask them how much loose change they think the whole class, including you, have now. Then get everyone to count the coins (but not any notes) in their pocket or wallet and write the amount on a small piece of paper – without their name on it. Collect all the pieces of paper and hand them to a student and ask him/her to add the amounts up. Ask the students, if someone gave them that amount of money now, what would they buy?

2. Show your students the list of expressions that you have created. Elicit from them what the expressions have in common (they are all related to money). Ask the students in turn to come up to the board and change the list by dragging an expression meaning having the least amount of money to the bottom of the screen and gradually placing the remaining expressions on top of each other to create a 'from rags to riches' list.
(**Key**: from top to bottom *to be made of money / to be loaded / to be well off, to make ends meet, to be in the red, to be strapped for cash, to be broke / to be bankrupt.* There is, however, more than one possible solution to the activity, since the first three expressions on the list are very similar to one another in meaning, as are the last two.)

Variation 1
Any collection of words or expressions that can be graded may be used for this kind of activity, for instance adverbs of frequency – *never, sometimes, frequently* etc. – or adjectives describing moods and feelings, such as *ecstatic, miserable, happy.*

3.4 From rags to riches

Variation 2

1. At elementary/beginner level, your students could also create lists addressing personalised issues such as:
   - irritating habits
   - what I like about weekends
   - favourite sports
   - favourite meals
   - things I am good at
   - my most treasured possessions.

2. Then invite your students to come up to the board to rearrange, add or remove the different contributions other students have made, to show how they would apply to them instead.

Vocabulary activities that involve analysing words and rearranging them according to different given criteria help learners commit those words to long-term memory.

Grammar ups and downs

Focus:	Reviewing grammar points
Level:	All
Time:	20 minutes
ICT skills:	None
Preparation:	1. Find or write about 15 to 20 sentences containing key grammar points appropriate to your students' language level. Make changes to some of the sentences in order to make them grammatically incorrect.
	2. Type each sentence on a different page of the board. Below each sentence, type either exactly the same sentence again if it was originally correct or, if it contained grammatical errors, a corrected version of it.
	3. Create a colour-filled rectangle to cover each second sentence.

in class

1. Set up three to five groups of students in the classroom. Give each group a piece of paper for them to draw on it a large arrow that can be clearly seen by the rest of the students from a distance. Tell the students to stand up in their groups and move as far as possible from each other group in the classroom, providing they can all see the board.

2. Show them the document on the board. Explain that you will be gradually showing sentences on the board. Some sentences are correct, some are not. In each group, the students will decide if each sentence displayed on the board is correct or incorrect. If correct, they must hold their piece of paper with the arrow pointing up. If incorrect, the arrow must be pointing down. Explain that you will give them 20 seconds per sentence to make a group decision and they cannot show their arrow until you tell them to. An accurate answer will earn them one point. The group with the most points at the end of the activity will win.

3. Reveal the first sentence. Give your students about 20 seconds to come to a decision. At the count of 3, all groups must show their piece of paper with the arrow pointing up or down. Drag away the rectangle covering the second sentence for students to check their answer.

4. Repeat Step 3 with the remaining sentences; keep a tally of the points.

3.5 Grammar ups and downs

Variation
Instead of grammar revision, you may choose phrasal verbs or idioms, or simply review general vocabulary.

Note
Get into the habit of keeping an updated list of your students' most common mistakes, and incorporate this authentic teaching material into your grammar ups and downs.

Students supporting each other towards a common goal reduces anxiety and increases self-confidence.

3.6 Google it

Focus: Searching for additional information on topics covered in class

Level: All

Time: Variable

ICT skills: Using search engines to browse for specific information

Preparation: After a reading / speaking session, invite your students to go online and look for additional information on the topic; ask them to rephrase or summarise the information they find, and email it to you to share with the class.

in class

1. Open the emails and show them on the board to elaborate on the topic with extra details or facts.

2. If too many students have contributed, making the activity too time-consuming, establish turns and designate a number of students that will contribute next time.

Variation
Ask your students to google specific words, phrases or language chunks that have come up in class. For instance, at an intermediate level, they could try googling "*on and off*", "*and so on*" or "*on and on*". Then they copy and paste a relevant example and email it to you to be opened in class the following day for revision.

Promote learner autonomy by showing students practical examples of how they can explore language on their own.

3.7 Hiding lyrics

Focus: Recalling song lyrics

Level: All

Time: 15 minutes

ICT skills: Creating, reproducing and resizing geometrical objects; dragging objects on the board; copying and pasting text

Preparation:
1. Write or type onto a page the lyrics of a song that you would like to play in class and use as part of your main lesson plan.
2. Copy and paste the document you have created onto another page.
3. Create a coloured rectangle long enough to cover the longest line on the second page. Copy it to produce as many rectangles as there are lines in the song. Cover each line with a rectangle, and number it.

in class

1. This activity is designed to take up the last 15 minutes or so of a lesson based on the song you have chosen.
2. Show your students the first page of your document with the full lyrics of the song. Tell them they have two minutes to observe it, and then you are going to hide it for them to play a game based on how much they can remember.
3. Go to the next page, where you placed the coloured rectangles covering the lyrics.
4. Set up two teams in your class (for example, boys vs. girls or people born between January–June vs. people born July–December).
5. The teams take turns to choose a numbered line and recall the words hidden under the rectangle; when they have come up with an answer, drag the rectangle off, for confirmation/correction. Award two points for successfully recalling a full line. If they need help, reveal a word or string of words and if they remember then, give them one point.

Variation 1
Instead of a song, use any other short written text, such as a newspaper article or a poem.

Variation 2
Instead of covering the lines with coloured rectangles, you may use the screen shade tool to gradually reveal the lines.

Language chunks are more easily learned, recognised and retrieved through the use of songs.

3.8 Just joking

Focus:	Providing additional details to text
Level:	Upper Intermediate–Advanced
Time:	20 minutes
ICT skills:	Editing text on the board; screen keyboard application
Preparation:	1. Find a joke which is appropriate for the class, reduce it to the bare minimum wording, and type it on the board. Three or four typed lines should be enough.
	2. Think of a few more jokes of a similar type.
	3. Open the screen keyboard application.

in class

1. Ask your class if they know any (appropriate) jokes in English. Invite them to share one or two jokes. If necessary, tell them some of those you have thought of.

2. Divide the class into five groups. Assign to each group one of the five senses: sight, hearing, taste, smell and touch.

3. Tell your groups that they are to add details to the joke by focussing on the sense they have been allotted. They can stay seated and use pen and paper.

4. Allow up to five minutes for your students to work in groups.

5. Invite your groups, in turns, to come up to the board. Ask them to double-click on the text, choose the Edit option from the pull-down menu and add their contributions. They may use the screen keyboard application or use the computer keyboard. In many cases, if not all, on top of adding details, they will have to make modifications to the original text. Provide help or elicit possible corrections for accurate use of English.

Variation 1
Instead of focussing on the five senses, you could ask your students to focus on grammar, such as adjectives, adverbs, nouns or verbs. This would be a more appropriate task with pre-intermediate to intermediate students.

Variation 2
You may also provide some relevant vocabulary beforehand.

Jokes release tension. They can also bring culture into the classroom and can serve as a stepping-stone for further meaningful activities.

CHAPTER 3: TEXT-BASED ACTIVITIES

3.9 Laser spelling

Focus:	Spelling troublesome words
Level:	All
Time:	5 minutes
ICT skills:	Laser pen tool
Preparation:	None

in class

1. Select a number of words that you have recently seen in class or that your students have trouble spelling.

2. For StarBoard users: Select the laser pen application on your board. Invite one of your students to come up to the board. Write one of your selected words on the board. As soon as you finish writing the word, touch anywhere on the board with your laser pen. This will make the word disappear.

3. Challenge your student to write the word.

4. Repeat Steps 2 and 3 as many times as words you selected.

Variation
For other brands: Instead of the laser pen, use the normal virtual pen. Set the colour to the background colour of the screen (usually white). Write the word on the board very slowly and using long traces. Nothing will show on the board. Challenge the student at the front to write the word you traced on the board, and everyone else to write it on paper. Change the colour setting for your student to write the word so it will stand out on the background. Then click on the word you wrote and change its colour to any other colour that will stand out against the background. The word you spelled will magically appear. Compare. You may turn this activity into a game and award points for correct words and spellings.

This activity will keep your students focussed and concentrating.

3.10 Magic dictionary

Focus: Reviewing vocabulary

Level: All

Time: 10 minutes

ICT skills: Creating, duplicating, grouping and layering objects

Preparation:

1. Choose 10 to 15 words that you would like to review in class.

2. Draw a solid black rectangle and resize it so that it fills the right-hand half of a page. Double-click on it and place it on the bottom layer of the page.

3. Open another page. Set the background colour to any colour but black or white, so that you will be able to see the words that you will be typing on it, in black and in white.

4. Type in black one of your words in the L1 language. Set the text colour to white and type the same word in the L2 language immediately after it (with no space between the two). For example, if L1 is Spanish, type "amigofriend" (with "amigo" in black and "friend" in white).

5. Repeat Step 4 for the remaining words.

6. Cut – or copy and paste – each set of paired words onto your first page. (Copying instead of cutting gives you the option of recycling the activity for future use by editing the words already created and re-using them). Align the words vertically on the left-hand side of the page. Only the L1 words – written in black – will be visible on the white background. When dragged to the right-hand side the L2 word will stand out on the black background and the L1 word will magically disappear.

in class

1. Open the document you have created. Your students will see a list of words in the L1 language on the left of the screen.

2. Invite students to come in turn to the board and select a word, ask the rest of the students for the L2 counterpart, then drag the word to the right-hand side for the L2 word to be revealed.

Variation 1
For higher-level classes, instead of single words, you may choose phrases or language chunks. These will need to be grouped.

3.10 Magic dictionary

Variation 2
For multilingual classes, instead of L1 words, make drawings and group them with the L2 words.

Produce new sets of words from time to time and keep the ones already created. Review both the 'old' and 'new' words for vocabulary reinforcement.

3.11 Moving phonemes

Focus: English phoneme sounds and transcriptions

Level: All

Time: 20 minutes

ICT skills: Dragging objects on the board

Preparation: Write all the English phonemes on the board, each one as an individual object for you and your students to drag. Place them in the top three-quarters of the screen.
Optional: find a website listing all the phonemes and their corresponding audio clips, e.g. www.bbclearningenglish.com. Hyperlink to the sound clips the phonemes you have written. Then each time you double-click on the phoneme in class, your students will hear the sound. This may be time-consuming but is worth the effort once it has been saved.

in class

1. Tell your students they are going to do work on the sounds of English and their phonemic transcriptions.

2. Show them the transcriptions that you have written on the board. Review them with the class and model the sounds.

3. Set up groups in class. Explain that you are going to select some phonemes for them to try to form English words. They can only use each selected phoneme once.

4. Select six vowel sounds and six consonant sounds, and drag them to the bottom of the screen.

5. Your students, in groups, try to form the longest word they can think of with the selected phonemes. Set up a time limit; about three minutes is suitable. Ask a student to come up to the board. As the groups call out the words they came up with, the student standing in front of the board will piece together the phonemes to build the word. Tell your students to keep a careful eye – and ear – open for possible mistakes.

6. Repeat Steps 4 and 5 as many times as you wish. Switch sounds at your convenience.

Variation 1
It is advisable to do this activity in small doses and gradually introduce the different phonemes of the language (especially when working with low-level classes). You may focus on specific sounds each time.

Constant exposure, repetition and recycling are needed for retention.

3.12 Multiple-choice story

Focus: Encouraging oral fluency: group improvisation of a spoken story

Level: Intermediate

Time: 20 minutes

ICT skills: None

Preparation: Open a blank page on the board and write three choices for the beginning of a story. Open a second page and write three further choices for the continuation of the story. Open a third page and write three additional choices, and so on. The choices on the last page you create should allow the story to continue from there. Here is an example with four pages:

Page 1:
- bank robber going to the bank
- film star (choose your own) going to the bank
- my next-door neighbour going to the bank

Page 2:
- wants to rob the bank
- wants to see his/her friend, who works at the bank
- wants to cash a cheque at the bank

Page 3:
- sees something suspicious
- the alarm goes off
- recognises someone she/he knows at the bank

Page 4:
- someone gets hurt at the bank
- a police officer happens to walk in
- something unexpected happens

in class

1. Ask your students: What do you think is the best way to tell a story? Through a novel, a poem, a song, a film? Are there any other ways of telling stories? Do you know any good stories told through those media, or any others?

2. Tell your class that they are going to create a story around some choices that they will be seeing on the board.

3. Show the first page of the document, and ask for someone to volunteer to start telling the story. He/She must choose one of the three options and provide some background details.

3.12 Multiple-choice story

4. Show the next page. Ask somebody else in the class to continue the story by choosing one of the three options and adding any details that spring to mind.

5. Repeat Step 4 with the remaining pages.

Extension 1
6. When all the pages have been shown, open a new blank page and elicit from your students three new options to write on it. Ask a student to choose one and, based on it, continue the story. Open a new blank page and elicit another set of three new options.

Extension 2
7. When all the pages have been shown, form groups in the class and ask each group to continue the story. Allow enough time for them to freely continue the story. Then ask each group to share the different chain of events.

Extension 3
8. Invite your students to send you emails from home with continuations of the story. Open the emails in class next time you see them, to share.

Empower your students by providing choices in the activities you devise.

3.13 Noughts and Crosses

Focus: Phrasal verbs review

Level: All

Time: 15–20 minutes

ICT skills: Creating and reproducing geometrical objects and dragging them on the board

Preparation:

1. Draw on the board a noughts and crosses grid (three rows and three columns). Make each square big enough for a phrasal verb to be written in it.

2. Create five red and four blue dots big enough to fit the squares.

3. Select the appropriate phrasal verbs you would like to introduce or review with your class, and write one in each of the squares on the board.

in class

1. Divide your class into two teams, red and blue. Tell the class they are about to play noughts and crosses. If necessary explain how to play the game – or, better, let a student do it.

2. Ask a member of the red team to choose a square; the team must produce a sentence to exemplify the use of the phrasal verb written in that square. If the team can produce a valid sentence within your time limit – say two minutes – drag a red dot onto that square. Otherwise, leave the phrasal verb uncovered. The blue team has a go now. Teams alternate. First team to place three dots in a row wins.

Variation 1
This game can accommodate almost any words or phrases. You may do general vocabulary revision, or jumble up the letters of the words placed in each square for the students to give you the correct spelling, or work on translation (from L1 to L2 or vice versa), or work on vocabulary for a specific semantic field, or deal with idioms or proverbs …

Variation 2
A more sophisticated and therefore more challenging activity would be for students to produce a conversation or dialogue based on the words selected. Thus, the red team must come up with a logical sentence using any word on the grid. Then the blue team's pick will result in a logical answer to the red team's sentence using the chosen word and so on. The teacher will be the judge, accepting or rejecting the conversation lines offered.

3.13 Noughts and Crosses

Variation 3
An option for large classes is to have more than two teams. Create a grid with more squares (six rows and six columns, for example), set up four or five groups and assign a different colour to each of them. First team to get three dots in a row wins. Otherwise, the team with the highest number of dots placed on the grid wins.

Charge your lessons with positive emotions by using games that are motivational and enjoyable.

3.14 Once upon a …

Focus: Recalling written text

Level: All

Time: 15 minutes

ICT skills: Copying and pasting text to a page

Preparation:
1. Find a reading passage that your students have already seen in class, preferably something they have just read.
2. Type or copy and paste the text – fully or partially – to a page.
3. Select the pen application, set the colour to the background colour of your screen and run the pen through the whole text, covering it completely.
4. Take a hard copy of the reading passage into class with you.

in class
1. Tell your students that they are going to review on the board the text they have just read. Open the document that you have created. Explain that, as you drag the virtual eraser on the board, the words will 'magically' appear.
2. Erase the ink over the first three or four words on the first line of the passage and ask your students to look at the screen and not at the passage in their books or handouts. Then elicit from them what they think the next word or words are. When your students give you a correct word or cluster of words, erase the virtual ink over it. If your students fail to give you an accurate answer for some time, give them a clue by revealing just one or two letters.

Variation
This activity also works very well with songs your students have just listened to.
Preparation: number the lines on your song and cover everything but the numbers with the virtual pen.
In class: divide your class into two groups: even and odd numbers. Then your groups take turns to tell you the hidden words on each line. Establish your own rules for the game, such as limiting the number of attempts for each line, giving bonus points for calling out the whole line at the first attempt, etc.

Revisiting texts and adding interaction with them will help grammar and vocabulary retention.

Personal profiles

Focus: Present simple tense

Level: Beginner–Elementary

Time: 15–20 minutes

ICT skills: Reproducing objects on the board; dragging objects on the board

Preparation:
1. Open a blank page and with the virtual pen write a list of ten statements about yourself – which may or may not be true – using the present simple tense in the third person singular. For instance, *Mr. Martin lives in Los Angeles* or *Mr. Martin usually goes to bed at 5 o'clock*. Leave ample space – at least a double space – between each sentence.

2. Next to each of your statements write TRUE and FALSE.

3. Draw a colour-filled rectangle big enough to cover the words TRUE and FALSE. Reproduce the square, making a total of twenty.

4. Cover each TRUE and FALSE word with a coloured rectangle.

in class

1. Tell your class that you are going to review the present simple tense, which is used to talk about daily routines, things we like or dislike, facts, etc. Explain that you are going to show on the screen ten statements about yourself that might or might not be true.

2. Open the document you have created. Start on the first statement, and ask them: *What do you think? Is it true or is it false? If you think it's true, raise your hand. Now, those who think it's false raise your hand.* Then drag the rectangle covering the correct answer out of the way to reveal it.

3. If the statement was false, ask a student to come up to the board and write a full statement below to correct it. For instance, *Mr. Martin doesn't usually go to bed at 5 o'clock*.

4. Repeat Steps 2 and 3 until the activity is completed.

5. Erase all the original sentences and corrections. Replace the rectangles over the TRUE and FALSE words.

3.15 Personal profiles

6. Ask the students to think of interesting sentences to write about themselves which might or might not be true, again using the third person singular and the present simple, e.g. *Tanya loves basketball.* Invite them to come up to the board and write their sentence in the space to the left of any available coloured rectangles.

7. Once you have ten new statements on the board, repeat Steps 2 and 3 again.

Variation 1
You could ask your students to do some research on a celebrity they like and write ten 'true or false' statements about him/her, and email the document to you. Open the document in class and follow the same plan as above.

Variation 2
The focal grammar point could be adapted to your class needs and level. Other possible options are the past simple, stating plans and ambitions with 'going to', describing habits with 'used to' etc.
You could also combine different elements, as in Step 3, which combines the present simple and the use of frequency adverbs. For more advanced classes, you could even try to 'personalise' idiomatic uses, such as *at my wits´ end; at the top of my voice* or *at odds*.

Arouse interest by bringing in personal meaning to the activities.

3.16 Personally speaking

Focus: Review of question forms (past, present and future)

Level: Elementary-Pre-intermediate

Time: 20 minutes

ICT skills: None

Preparation: Open a blank page. Write PAST at the top. Open another page. Write PRESENT at the top. Open a third page. Write FUTURE at the top.

in class

1. Tell your students that you are going to review question forms with them and you want them to think of questions about your personal life that they might like to ask you. The questions could be about your past, present or future. They are free to ask anything in good taste – and you are free to turn down some of the questions, if they are too personal.

2. Show them the three pages that you have created. As they think of questions, they should come up to the board, scroll through the pages if needed and write their question on the right page. Limit the questions to ten per page.

3. Have an overall review of the questions to clarify meaning and to correct possible mistakes. Elicit from your students the corrections for any mistakes.

4. Start on PAST and move forwards, sharing your life experiences as you answer the questions.

Extension 1
5. Set up groups for students to think of questions to ask each other, and distribute index cards or small pieces of paper for your students to write questions on them.

Extension 2
6. Ask your class to write a brief profile on you based on the information that they have gathered.

Variation 1
To spice things up and to get extra attention, you could let your students know that in each page you are going to include one lie in your answers. Encourage them to be attentive in order to see if they can spot the lie.

Consider using this activity for the first day of the school year.

3.17 Pop lines

Focus: Producing short dialogues using song titles

Level: Pre-intermediate–Upper Intermediate

Time: 20 minutes

ICT skills: Browsing online

Preparation: Find a website listing the current pop music hits. For example, you could try www.billboard.com or www.bbc.co.uk/radio1/chart/. Open a blank page and insert a hyperlink to the selected website.

in class

1. Ask your class which pop songs are popular at the moment. Ask them if anyone has with them an MP3 player or a mobile phone with songs in it. Which songs do they have? When and where do they listen to music?

2. Show your students the pop music chart that you have selected. Do they recognise any of the songs? Perhaps they can sing some lines.

3. Set up groups of two to four students and ask them to write mini dialogues using actual song titles from the ones they can see on the board. Allow a few minutes, and circulate to provide help.

4. The groups, in turns, read out their dialogues.

Variation
Run a search online for popular songs. List on the board the song titles. Invite your students to come up to the board, select the titles and arrange them to form dialogues.

A fun way to explore language.

152　　CHAPTER 3: TEXT-BASED ACTIVITIES

3.18 Predicting answers

Focus: Predicting factual information from reading passages

Level: Intermediate–Advanced

Time: 25 minutes

ICT skills: Copying and pasting text to a page

Preparation:
1. Find a short news article online suitable for your students' language level and interest. Copy and paste it to a page. You may need to highlight the whole text and enlarge the size for better visibility.

2. Open a new page in the same document. Type the headline and create a numbered list of statements, phrases or words from the article that contain factual information. Select the pen application, set the colour to the same background colour on your screen and run the pen through the answers, covering everything except the numbers.

in class

1. Tell your students that you have selected a news article for them. Show the second page of the document and focus on the headline. Ask your students if they can guess any information in the article by looking at the headline.

2. Invite a student to come up to the board, select the eraser application and rub the eraser to the right of one of the numbers on the board (the eraser will erase the digital ink covering the text, but not the text itself). A word or phrase will appear.

3. The students generate possible questions for that answer.

4. Repeat Steps 2 and 3 until all the hidden words have been unveiled.

5. Ask your students (in groups) to write a short text, as if they were reproducing the news story, using the information gathered so far.

6. Invite all or a few groups to read their texts.

7. Show the news article on the first page. Compare.

3.18 Predicting answers

Here is an example:

Confused sea turtles march into restaurant
About 60 newly hatched sea turtles lost their way during their ritual passage to the sea and marched into an Italian restaurant instead, a conservation worker said on Monday.

The baby turtles — which ended up under the tables of startled diners at the beachside restaurant — were probably thrown off track and lured by the eatery's bright lights, said Antonio Colucci, who was called to help rescue the group.

"They saw the artificial lights and took the wrong route," said Colucci, who works on a turtle monitoring project for the conservation group WWF (World Wide Fund for Nature).

"The diners were at first quite curious and then someone alerted the coastal authorities."

The stranded turtles, which had hatched on a beach in the southern Italian region of Calabria, were released into the sea.

Female sea turtles nest on beaches and their offspring instinctively head to the sea after hatching from their eggs.

Source: uk.news.yahoo.com

Hidden phrases for the second page:

1. About 60
2. Under the tables
3. They saw the artificial lights
4. At first quite curious
5. Were released into the sea

Variation
Choose a reading comprehension passage from your textbook or some other source, or even a listening comprehension transcript.

Forming a mental picture prior to reading contributes to a better understanding and greater interaction with the text.

Question, please

Focus: Writing questions based on song lyrics; interpreting and discussing song lyrics

Level: Intermediate–Advanced

Time: 20–30 minutes

ICT skills: Copying and pasting text

Preparation:

1. Write down or copy onto the upper half of a page the lyrics of a song that you would like your students to listen to in class.

2. Draw a rectangle to fill the bottom half of the page, and head it with the words *Questions, please*.

3. Optional: you could get the list started by thinking up and writing a few thought-provoking questions suitable to the nature of the song and the class language level.

in class

1. Show the lyrics on the board and encourage your students to come up to the board and write questions about the song. They should feel free to write vocabulary-based questions, or questions focusing on what happens in the story in the song, or about issues or interpretations raised in their mind by the lyrics.

2. Set up groups in your class. The students discuss the questions in groups.

3. The groups share their discussions.

Have your students create their own questions for the reading or listening materials you bring to class.

3.20 Sentence patterns

Focus: Present perfect continuous

Level: Pre-intermediate–Intermediate

Time: 10–15 minutes

ICT skills: Dragging objects on the board

Preparation: Create the following chart on the top half of a page. Make sure that each word /phrase can be dragged out of its box.

I You you It it He he She she We we They they	Have have Haven't haven't Has has Hasn't hasn't	been	learning speaking cutting cleaning playing driving	a car the grass English Chinese football the house	for ages yet since May for an hour all day long all my life	. ?

in class

1. Show the class the document you have created.

2. Drag one of each type of language unit out of the grid and piece them together to form a grammatically correct sentence. Drag the words back into the grid again.

3. Invite a student to form a new sentence.

4. Repeat Step 3 as many times as you consider convenient. Make sure you practise positive and negative statements as well as question forms.

5. Invite your students to add more words or phrases to the fourth and fifth columns.

6. Continue forming more sentences with your students.

Variation
Use the same procedure for teaching or practising other language items such as verb forms, placement of adjectives and adverbs in English or use of the passive voice.

Interactive whiteboards are a great tool for tactile learners.

3.21 Song poems

Focus: Encouraging creative use of the language

Level: All

Time: 15 minutes

ICT skills: None

Preparation:

1. Find a song that you would like to play in class, and ensure you have the equipment to do this.

2. Make a selection of key words or small language chunks from the song, and type them on the board. Place them randomly on the upper three quarters of the page, leaving some space at the bottom to write into.

in class

1. Tell your class that you have typed a few words and phrases on the board for them to write short poems. Ask them in groups to write a short poem (around four to eight lines) using as many of the words on the board as they want. They may also add any other words of their own. Allow about five minutes, and circulate to provide help if needed.

2. Invite all your groups to read out their poems.

3. Your students vote on the poem they liked the best.

4. The author of the selected poem writes it on the board.

5. Ask the students to copy down on a piece of paper the poem they can see on the board. Tell them that the language that you wrote on the board is actually contained in a song that you are about to play. They will have to try to identify how many of the word combinations in the poem, that is two or more words together, are actually present in the song.

Variation
Instead of a song use a poem, and at Step 5 read it out to your class.

Promote activities with open-ended questions.

3.22 Sounds like it

Focus:	Phonemes of the English language
Level:	All
Time:	15 minutes
ICT skills:	Dragging objects on the board
Preparation:	1. Find common clusters of vowels that represent specific sounds of the English language and list them on the left side of the board. An example for the /i:/ sound would be: – ee – eo – ea – e – ie – ei – ey – i

2. Write down a variety of phonetically transcribed English words containing the specific sounds in the clusters above in any order. For instance: /si:/, /tri:/, /stri:t/, /fri:/, /´pi:pəl/, /ri:d/, /mi:t/, /´li:də/, /ti:/ /ði:z/, /ʃi:/, /wi:/, /fi:ld/, /bə´li:v/, /pi:s/, /rə´si:v/, /ki:/, /mə´ʃi:n/, /pə´li:s/ (the corresponding words being *see, tree, street, free, people, read, meat, leader, tea, these, she, we, field, believe, peace, receive, key, machine, police*). Place them on the right side of the board.

in class

1. Open the document you have created. Ask your students what all those clusters of vowels have in common.

2. Invite your students to come up to the board, select the phonetic transcriptions on the right-hand side and match them with their corresponding vowels on the left. Additionally, ask them to spell out in writing those transcriptions.

3. Ask your students if they can think of any other words with an /i:/ sound to match the vowels on the left. Let them add those words to the list.

4. Model the pronunciation of each word and encourage choral repetition.
Invite them to send you emails – or write down on paper – short poems using words that rhyme with the ones seen in class.

3.22 Sounds like it

Note
This is a possible way to gradually introduce – or review – the sounds of English. As you eventually build up a collection of clusters of letters and phonetically transcribed words, copy and paste them onto one page to recycle previous sounds. These are some websites where you can find useful material:
www.bbc.co.uk/worldservice/learningenglish/grammar/pron
www.esltower.com/pronunciation.html
www.phon.ucl.ac.uk/home/johnm/flash/flashin.htm
http://international.ouc.bc.ca/pronunciation
www.uiowa.edu/~acadtech/phonetics/english/frameset.html
www.shiporsheep.com
www.ugoeigo.com

Words have weight, sound and appearance; it is only by considering these that you can write a sentence that is good to look at and good to listen to. (William Somerset Maugham)

3.23 Taking sides grammar

Focus: Use of articles in English

Level: Beginner–Intermediate

Time: 40 minutes

ICT skills: Dragging objects on the board

Preparation:

1. Find grammar notes suited to your students' level in your textbook or grammar book, or on the internet, or use your own notes on the use of articles in English. If your students will not be using a book, print copies for them.

2. Open a blank page and write the grammar notes as isolated sentences placed at random on the board.

3. Make changes to some of those grammar notes to make them untrue. For example, if the original sentence reads *do not use an article before a noun when talking in general terms*; change it into *you must use an article before a noun when talking in general terms*.

in class

1. Hand out copies of your grammar notes or ask your students to open their books on the required page. Tell them that they have eight minutes to read and understand the information there. They do not need to memorise anything. Circulate to provide help.

2. Ask your students to put away their notes or put their books down. Open the document you have created. Mention that some of the notes on the board are untrue.

3. Call a student to the front and ask him/her to choose a sentence from the board, click on it and drag it all the way to the right if he/she thinks the sentence is accurate or all the way to the left if inaccurate.

4. Ask the class if they agree with the student's decision. They must take sides; to agree they must put their thumbs up, and to disagree, thumbs down. With smaller groups you may ask them to move to different corners of the classroom (label them as Agree and Disagree) depending on their choice.

5. Reveal the correct answer.

3.23 Taking sides grammar

6. If the original sentence was true, ask if anyone in the class can think of a sentence that can illustrate that particular grammar point. Encourage them to write it on the board. If correct, keep that sentence on the board and drag it next to that particular grammar note.

7. Repeat Steps 3 to 6 until you run out of sentences.

Variation 1
This activity can easily be adapted to any language level depending on the difficulty level and nature of the grammar point.

Variation 2
Instead of grammar notes, you can use example sentences for your students to decide if they contain mistakes or not.

Variation 3
Collect samples of writing from your students that contain mistakes, and mix them with samples that show accurate use of English. This is an excellent opportunity for them to review their most common mistakes. Be diplomatic, choosing samples from many students to review rather than taking most sentences from students who make a large number of errors.

Make provision for action in grammar activities to fully engage your students.

3.24 Taking sides maze

Focus:	Reading comprehension; encouraging speaking interaction
Level:	All
Time:	20 minutes
ICT skills:	Copying and pasting text (optional); scanning documents (optional)
Preparation:	1. Find a text maze for your students to read in class. (If you are not familiar with them, text mazes are stories that pose a series of situations in response to each of which readers are given a choice of two or three actions to take. Each choice tells the reader to turn to another page in the book or to pick up a card, which in turn will prompt more actions to choose from and so on. Text mazes usually lead to either a happy or a disastrous ending.) These are some websites where you can find text mazes: www.elrebumbio.org/materialasist/materquandary/village.htm www.stclaresenglish.net/mazes-intro.htm www.grahamstanley.com/englishfortourism/units/010/mazes.html www.actionmazes.com/
	2. If your maze is not in digital form but printed on paper or cards, you will have to copy the text, as shown in the printed version, onto your different pages. Alternatively, you may scan the texts. (It is time-consuming to type or even scan a substantial amount of text, but worthwhile, as it can be used and recycled over and over again.) If your maze is in digital form, simply copy and paste it. Each card or text passage should be on a different page of your document, numbered the same as the original you're using, and you need to create a hyperlink between each numbered option and the page it leads to.

in class

1. Ask your class for the meaning of the word 'maze'. Ask them if they have ever worked their way through a text maze in an English class.

2. Create ample space in two corners of your classroom, and make and place the following signs in them: First Option / Second Option. If some pages of your maze provide more than two choices, make additional signs for those options and place them in other corners.

3. Tell the students that you are going to show a text maze on the board. Display the first page. Ask them to all decide which corner they want to go to, and allow sufficient time for them to make a decision. Students walk to the corresponding corner.

3.24 Taking sides maze

4. Ask your students to explain their choice. Encourage volunteering, or ask randomly. Some possible questions – depending on the nature of the problem posed – could be: *Why did you decide to go over there? Which are the pros and cons of your decision? What do you think is going to happen now? Why don't you agree with the choice that the people over there made?* Ask the other group/s the same or similar questions.

5. Count the number of people in each corner/s. The option chosen by the greatest number of people will prevail. Turn to the page indicated by that option.

6. Repeat Steps 3, 4 and 5 until you reach a final outcome to the story.

Variation
As a long-term project, you could ask your students to write their own text mazes once they are familiar with the way they are structured. You could assign individual or group projects. The maze could centre on a particular topic you would like your students to be engaged in, such as school, work, money, relationships, etc.

Quandary is a shareware application that generates web-based action mazes. Download site: www.halfbakedsoftware.com/quandary_download.php

This activity is very helpful for student bonding.

3.25 Text puzzle

Focus: Paragraphing

Level: All

Time: 15 minutes

ICT skills: Using the screen capture tool

Preparation:

1. Find a short reading passage with a sequence of events. Copy and paste – or type – the text into a page.

2. Open the screen capture application. Take a snapshot of each paragraph on the board.

3. Move each snapshot to a random area of the board.

4. Cut and paste the original reading passage to another page, as a key.

in class

1. Show your class the document you have created.

2. Invite your students to come up to the board in turn, to select a paragraph and place them in order, thus reconstructing the story.

A quick way to prepare reading activities to work on text structure and organisation.

Top ten

Focus: Present continuous for arranged events

Level: Elementary

Time: 15 minutes

ICT skills: Creating, reproducing and dragging objects on the board

Preparation:
1. Open a blank page and create a list of ten things, authentic or invented, that you are planning to do this weekend. Use the present continuous for all your sentences; to emphasise that verb tense, change the colour of its letters within the sentence, or use the highlighter pen on your board, or use a larger font.

2. Create a coloured rectangle long enough to cover the longest sentence. Make nine copies of that rectangle. Place each rectangle over a sentence, to cover them all. (Make sure you remember where everything is, or print out a copy of the uncovered sentences for yourself, or write them down on a piece of paper).

in class

1. Tell your students that you are looking forward to the weekend since it is going to be very eventful. Puzzle them a little bit. Ask them if they have any plans.

2. Show them the document you have created and explain that you want them to guess what ten activities you have hidden; elicit spontaneous answers.

3. Drag the coloured rectangles out of the way as your students make correct guesses.

4. If your students are finding it difficult to guess correctly, help them out by moving a coloured rectangle so they can see part of the sentence.

5. Once all the coloured rectangles have been removed, take a few minutes to elaborate on the grammar use.

6. Ask your students to create their own top ten lists, and pair them so that they can make guesses.

Variation 1
This activity can be adapted to any grammatical point and any language level. You can use it for introducing your grammar explanation or for further practice and review. Other possible top ten lists are:
Things I used to do when I was six ('used to' for past habits).

3.26 Top ten

My ten ambitions in life ('want to', 'would like to', 'looking forward to', 'wish', 'expect').
Things I did over the weekend (past simple).
Things I would do if I won the lottery (conditional).
Things you can do to improve your English (expressing advice).

Variation 2
You may also use this technique for recycling vocabulary. Ask your students to open a blank page on a word processor and create two columns, one with their top ten words or expressions learned so far, and another one with the equivalent definitions or explanations, and email you the attached document, to use instead. (If you do this 'live', ask the students, when you open the document, to close their eyes or look down so you can cover the words and expressions on the left.)

Grammar should also address personal experiences and emotions.

Walk this way

Focus: Verbs describing ways of walking

Level: Advanced

Time: 10 minutes

ICT skills: None

Preparation:
1. Make a selection of verbs that describe different ways of walking that you would like to introduce or review in class. Some verbs that could be suitable for this language level are: *limp, hobble, stagger, tiptoe, stroll, wander, stride, strut, trudge, stump, pace, march, sneak, prowl, dash, hike.*

2. Write down each verb on a different page on your board, followed by the corresponding definition.

in class

1. Introduce or review the verbs with your students. You may show the pages on the board with the definitions.

2. Click on the thumbnails button on your board, so a little window will open displaying the pages of the document.

3. Invite all your students to stand up. Click on any of the thumbnails to show any given page with a verb and a definition. Your students should walk around the room in that way.

4. After a few seconds, click on a different thumbnail for your students to walk in the way shown on that page. Repeat this process a few more times, displaying a different verb each time.

Variation
Record very short videos where you can show the different ways of walking, and hyperlink those videos to the pages with the verbs and definitions/explanations. That way, when you click on the thumbnails you add a video component to the activity. If you intend to show a short video, digital cameras are normally easier to operate than camcorders in terms of transferring and handling files.

**Caminante, no hay camino,
Se hace camino al andar. (Antonio Machado)
(Traveller, there is no road,
You make your own road by walking.)**

3.28 What a holiday!

Focus: Writing about holidays; coached writing

Level: Beginner–Elementary

Time: 15 minutes

ICT skills: None

Preparation: Type the following text on the board leaving enough space in the gaps for your students to fill them in in handwriting (sometimes one word, sometimes several, sometimes a complete sentence):

> Dear Sarah and Michael,
>
> Having a ………………… time. The weather here is ………………… . It's ………………… every day. We are so …………………! The hotel is ………………… . Our room is ………………… and the beach …………………
> but ………………….
>
> See you soon,
>
> Your friend.

in class

1. Lead into this activity by asking your students to tell you about the worst holiday they ever had. Why was it so bad? Enquire also about the best one, and ask them what made it so memorable. Help them with the vocabulary needed. For beginners you may ask these questions in the L1.

2. Set up small groups in your class and project the skeleton story onto the board. Tell your groups that they have to imagine they are having either a fantastic or a disastrous holiday. Allow enough time for them to copy down the skeleton story on a piece of paper and fill in each gap with as many words as they wish, as long as the final writing sample is grammatically correct and is also consistent with the choice they made.

3. Invite a group of students to come up to the board, fill in the gaps and share their work.

4. Invite another group. Ask them to erase what has been written, and fill in the gaps with their own words.

5. Repeat Steps 3 and 4 a few more times.

3.28 What a holiday!

Variation 1
If you do not wish to erase your students´ contributions, copy and paste the skeleton story onto as many pages as groups who will be writing on the board. Then work through the pages as the groups come up to the board.

Variation 2
Create your own writing skeleton, depending on your students´ language level and interests. A highly interesting and creative activity using writing skeletons is the production of poems.

Variation 3
A less time-consuming variation in terms of preparation is to use writing material from your textbook. Type the sample on the board, leaving gaps at your discretion.

Develop reading skills and vocabulary production in context.

3.29 What's cooking?

Focus: Verbs commonly used in instructions for food recipes

Level: Intermediate

Time: 15 minutes

ICT skills: Copying and pasting pictures and text

Preparation:
1. Find a recipe online for your students to see in class.
2. Copy and paste the recipe, and a picture of the finished dish, too. Enlarge the text as much as possible.
3. Create a colour-filled rectangle wide and long enough to completely cover the longest line of text on the screen. Duplicate the rectangle as many times as there are lines contained in the text, and cover each line with a rectangle so that no text is visible.

in class
1. Ask your students whether or not they like cooking, and what their favourite dishes are. Have they ever tried any international dishes at an ethnic restaurant? What did they have for lunch or dinner yesterday? Add any other food-related questions you can think of.
2. Introduce or review key vocabulary for food recipes and/or key vocabulary contained in the recipe you selected.
3. Open the document you have created. Your students will see the picture of the dish and the rectangles covering the lines of the text. Explain that the recipe is hidden behind the rectangles.
4. Drag the first rectangle sideways to the right to reveal the first full sentence. Drag the next rectangle too, just enough to reveal the word or words leading up to a verb, but do not show the verb. Invite your students to make educated guesses as to what verb it might be.
5. Every time a correct guess is made, drag the rectangle along again to reveal and confirm the verb, and continue moving it to the right until you get to the next verb.

Variation
Find some factual information about a well-known person, including past simple and present perfect verb tenses.

Consolidate knowledge in small doses.

3.30 What did Lydia do yesterday?

Focus:	Irregular past tense
Level:	Elementary
Time:	10 minutes
ICT skills:	None
Preparation:	1. Select a few verbs with an irregular past tense that you would like to introduce or review with your class.
	2. Open a blank page and write a sentence with each of those verbs using one of your students´ names (for instance, *Lydia went shopping yesterday; Lydia bought an English dictionary yesterday; Lydia sent me an email yesterday*; and so on). Write each sentence on a different page.

in class

1. Ask your students, in pairs, to tell each other what they did yesterday.

2. Bring a student to the front of the class with his/her back to the board. Open the document you have created.

3. Tell this student that Lydia did a lot of things yesterday. He or she should try to guess what Lydia did by looking at the rest of the students, who will be miming the expressions displayed on the board.

4. Display the first expression. Invite all your students to stand up and mime what they see. The student at the front may make as many guesses as he/she wishes until he/she gets the right answer. Advance to the next page and repeat.

Variation 1
You may invite four students to come to the front, and then run a competition (the first person to guess correctly stays at the front, to be joined by three more students and so on until a winner emerges). If you have time, you could bring back the winners of earlier rounds to challenge the winner of the last round.

Variation 2
Your students could work in small groups. Ask half the members of each group to close their eyes for a few seconds while you display a sentence. Ask the remaining students to look at the board and memorise the sentence. Then erase the sentence, ready for them to start miming.

3.30 What did Lydia do yesterday?

Variation 3
The focus of your lesson could be on regular past tense pronunciation. If that is the case, think of sentences where you can include the appropriate verb (for instance, you can focus on /–id/ pronunciation in sentences such as *Lydia started a blog yesterday; Lydia needed to go to the doctor yesterday; Lydia wanted to watch the football game on television yesterday but the TV broke down*, etc.). And of course this technique can be used with any other grammar point (conditionals, future, passive voice, reporting verbs, etc.).

Positive images in the mind reduce the fear of making errors.

Useful Resources

- www.tre.ngfl.gov.uk Teacher Resource Exchange: moderated database of resources and activities created by teachers.

- www2.smarttech.com Support, training and resources for Smartboard interactive board users.

- http://www.youtube.com/SMARTclassrooms Videos for Smartboard interactive board users.

- www.prometheanplanet.com / www.prometheanworld.com Support, training and resources for Promethean interactive board users.

- starboard.hitachi-software.co.uk Support, training and resources for Starboard interactive board users.

- www.easiteach.com Interactive teaching software for all whiteboards.

- www.interactive-whiteboards.co.uk Free interactive whiteboard guide and comparison charts.

- www.becta.org.uk British Educational Communications and Technology.

- www.mirandanet.ac.uk ICT in education.

- www.languages-ict.org.uk Information and guidance for language teachers on using ICT in the classroom.

- www.teachersfirst.com/whiteboard.cfm Resources for using interactive whiteboards.

- www.teachernet.gov.uk Education site for teachers and school managers.

- www.cardiffschools.net/~roelmann/whiteboard A wealth of resources for the interactive whiteboard.

- www.teachers.tv Thousands of education programs, including coverage of interactive whiteboards.

- www.iwbskills.com Interactive whiteboard resources

- www.wmnet.org.uk Interactive whiteboard resources.

- www.bgfl.org/bgfl/15.cfm Interactive whiteboard resources.

- www.echalk.co.uk Interactive whiteboard resources.

- www.iwb.org.uk Interactive whiteboard resources.

Useful Resources

- www.interactivewhiteboard.net.au Interactive whiteboard news, resources and advice.

- www.think-bank.com/iwb Interactive whiteboard resources.

- www.smart-education.org Classroom resources for the interactive board.

- www.activboarding.blogspot.com Blog on interactive whiteboards in education.

- www.iwb-efl.blogspot.com Blog on interactive whiteboards and English as a foreign language.

- http://groups.diigo.com/groups/iwb-pedgagogy Group to discuss, collaborate and share IWB pedagogical research, resources and projects.

- http://groups.diigo.com/groups/interactive-whiteboards-in-the-classroom Internet group for interactive whiteboard users.

- http://whiteboardchallenge.wikispaces.com Collaborative website for iwb ideas and challenges.

- www.blog-efl.blogspot.com Observations on the use of Web 2.0 tools for English language teaching and learning.

- www.interactivewhiteboards.blogspot.com Tips on choosing an interactive whiteboard.

- www.whiteboardblog.co.uk Interactive whiteboard blog.

- www.ros.org.uk/iwb Interactive whiteboard research forum.

- www.whiteboardweb.co.uk Online whiteboard forum.

- www.pdtogo.com/smart Smartboard lessons podcast.

Teacher's quick-reference guide

This guide will help you select an activity suitable for your class based on the time you have available, your own ICT expertise and the learning level(s) of your students.

To use it, look down the left-hand column till you come to a time that's right for you. In the next column is an indication of the ICT skill level needed, and if that suits you as well, look across to see the focus of the activity spread across the range of language levels it fits. When you've found something that matches your needs, look in the right-hand column to find the activity number and name.

Or if you prefer to start with the level of your students, go downwards till you find an activity focus, and on that same row you will find the time and ICT skill level required, and the activity number and name.

Please note, however, that the time guide is very approximate; it does not take account of any extension. It merely allows you to see, when you're thinking of running an activity for the first time, how long the activity is *likely* to take. When you look at the details of the activity, you may find that the time is more flexible than appears in this guide.

Teacher's quick-reference guide

Lesson time (mins)	ICT skill level *	Beginner	Elementary	Upper elementary	Pre-inter-mediate	Inter-mediate	Upper in-termediate	Advanced	Activity no and name
Chapter 1 – Image-based activities									
5	N	Present continuous							1.35 What's happening?
10	N	Indoor objects vocabulary; there is / there are, there was / there were							1.9 Flashing pictures
10	N		Asking and giving directions						1.14 How do I get to …?
10	N	Present simple							1.28 Similar but different
10	N				Writing about advantages and disadvantages				1.31 The good side/the bad side
10	N					English for jobs			1.32 The importance of English
10	N		Weather expressions						1.34 Weather report
10	N	Adverbs of frequency							1.15 How often?
10	I				Predictions; may, might, could be, looks like				1.19 More than meets the eye
10	I	Classroom objects vocabulary							1.21 My ideal classroom
10	I				Structuring guesses in English				1.26 Puzzled!
10	I	Everyday objects vocabulary							1.36 What's in there?
10–15	N	Present continuous							1.18 Mime the picture
10–20	I		General speaking practice and intonation						1.16 In the picture
15	N		Daily routines; sequencing events						1.1 A day in the life of …
15	N					Encouraging speaking fluency			1.2 A story in pictures
15	N		Contrasting and comparing pictures; formulating associations						1.3 Associations
15	N	Asking questions, physical descriptions							1.7 Face to face
15	N				Speaking fluency- connections and associations				1.23 Picture dominoes
15	N						Reviewing idioms		1.24 Picture idioms
15	N	Present simple							1.25 Picture it
15	N		Stress patterns in works						1.29 Stress patterns
15	N		Speaking fluency – adding details to a story						1.33 Unfolding story
15	N						Describing landscapes		1.38 Wish you were here
15	I	Comparisons							1.8 Find the differences
15	I	Classroom objects vocabulary							1.27 Silent bingo
15	I		Comparisons						1.30 Tall-taller-the tallest
15–20	I	Prepositions of place							1.37 Where's Johnny?

* ICT skill levels: N = novice, I = intermediate, A = advanced

Teacher's quick-reference guide

Lesson time (mins)	ICT skill level *	Beginner	Elementary	Upper elementary	Pre-intermediate	Intermediate	Upper intermediate	Advanced	Activity no and name
Chapter 1 – Image-based activities									
20	N		Language in situations: eating out						1.4 At a restaurant
20	N		Vocabulary review; word associations; how things are related						1.6 Connections
20	N		Travelling by plane						1.11 Going places
20	N			Speaking fluency					1.12 Happy birthday to you!
20	N				Asking questions, describing objects, speaking fluency				1.20 Most treasured possession
30	I					Reviewing idioms based on animals			1.13 Horsing around
30–40	N					Asking questions, speaking fluency			1.5 Blind date
40	N				Buying tickets, ordering food, shopping				1.22 Out and about
40–60	N				Numbers 1,000–10,000,000				1.10 Going, going, gone!
60	N					Class debates, future forms			1.17 Life in 2050
Chapter 2 – Sound and video-based activities									
5	I		Reading practice; song lines						2.7 DIY Karaoke
10	N					Describing actions			2.19 Silent film
10	I	Stress patterns + intonation							2.11 Hummed greetings
10	A		Vocabulary review						2.4 Concentration
15	N		Phonetics, discriminating sounds						2.17 Odd words
15	I		Reading practice, vocabulary review						2.6 Disappearing lines
15	I					Football-related terms			2.13 It's football time
15	I					Intonation / moods			2.16 Moody sounds
15	I	Personal descriptions, family members							2.21 Sounds familiar
15	A				Intonation in sentences				2.12 Intonation patterns
15	A		Pronunciation, stress, intonation						2.10 Film dubbers
15–20	I		Listening practice						2.1 Audio puzzle
20	A		Writing dialogues						2.3 Bubble story
20	I					Reporting verbs for reported speech			2.18 Reporting verbs
20	I				Sequencing events; creating a story around pictures				2.22 Still frames
20	I				Vocabulary recall				2.23 Talking categories

* ICT skill levels: N = novice, I = intermediate, A = advanced

Teacher's quick-reference guide

Lesson time (mins)	ICT skill level *	Beginner	Elementary	Upper elementary	Pre-inter-mediate	Inter-mediate	Upper in-termediate	Advanced	Activity no and name
Chapter 2 – Sound and video-based activities									
20	I	Vocabulary review							2.26 Videoclip quiz
20	N	Word order							2.14 Jumbled-up song lines
25	I					Class debates			2.5 Controversial issues
30	N	Writing narratives, adding details, editing							2.9 Expanding stories
30–40	N	Sequencing; listening to and understanding audiovisual learning materials							2.8 Every film tells a story
30–40	I						Predicting words		2.25 Video auction
35	I	Recognising and sequencing song lyrics							2.15 Karaoke makers
40	I				Predicting information; generating questions; watching and understanding news stories					2.24 The newsroom
40	A						Video-based comprehension questions		2.20 Snakes and ladders online news
40–60	N				Anticipating relevant focal vocabulary; listening to and understanding authentic news stories					2.2 Breaking news
50	I				Encouraging oral fluency; listening to authentic material; writing dialogues					2.27 Whose line is it?
Chapter 3 – Text-based activities									
5	N	Spelling troublesome words							3.9 Laser spelling
10	N							Ways of walking	3.27 Walk this way
10	N		Irregular past tense						3.30 What did Lydia do yesterday?
10	I	Reviewing vocabulary							3.10 Magic dictionary
10–15	N					Present perfect continuous			3.20 Sentence patterns
15	N					Booking a flight			3.2 Flying places
15	N	Word order; encouraging language creativity							3.3 Fridge magnets
15	N					Expressions used to talk about having or lacking money			3.4 From rags to riches
15	N	Reading practice; recalling song lyrics							3.7 Hiding lyrics
15	N	Recalling written text							3.14 Once upon a …
15	N	Encouraging creative use of the language							3.21 Song poems
15	N	Phonemes							3.22 Sounds like it
15	N	Paragraphing							3.25 Text puzzle

* ICT skill levels: N = novice, I = intermediate, A = advanced

Teacher's quick-reference guide

Lesson time (mins)	ICT skill level *	Beginner	Elementary	Upper elementary	Pre-intermediate	Intermediate	Upper intermediate	Advanced	Activity no and name
Chapter 3 – Text-based activities									
15	N			Present continuous for arranged events					3.26 Top ten
15	N	Writing about holidays; coached writing							3.28 What a holiday!
15	N					Cooking-related terms, verbs for recipes			3.29 What's cooking?
15–20	N	Phrasal verbs review							3.13 Noughts and crosses
15–20	N	Present simple							3.15 Personal profiles
20	N						Adding to text		3.8 Just joking
20	N	Phoneme sounds and transcriptions							3.11 Moving phonemes
20	N					Oral fluency: improvising a story			3.12 Multiple-choice story
20	N		Reviewing question forms: past, present, future						3.16 Personally speaking
20	N				Producing short dialogues using song titles				3.17 Pop lines
20	N	Reading comprehension; encouraging speaking interaction							3.24 Taking sides maze
20	I	Reviewing grammar points							3.5 Grammar ups and downs
20–30	N						Reviewing words and expressions used to give views on books		3.1 Avid readers
20–30	N					Writing questions based on song lyrics; interpreting and discussing song lyrics			3.19 Question, please
25	N					Predicting factual information from reading passages			3.18 Predicting answers
40	N	Use of articles							3.23 Taking sides grammar
Variable	N	Searching for additional information on topics covered in class							3.6 Google it

* ICT skill levels: N = novice, I = intermediate, A = advanced

The CD-ROM

The CD-ROM accompanying this book has 24 activities.

All the activities are included in the book and are ready to use in class with your interactive whiteboard.

 The IW icon and the specific activity pages flags when the activity is available on the CD-ROM.

This CD-ROM can be played directly from your computer.